NEAT

Little

ROWS

'The Black Country Grenadier'

BY

ANDREW MARK RUDALL

~ A Rad-Boo-Diddle Press Publication ~

Neat Little Rows

Entirely self-published by the author

REVISION - 002
FIRST PUBLISHED 22 APRIL 2012

Cover design by Adison Rudall - www.thisisbold.co.uk
Book format and layout by the author

ISBN: 978-1-4716-4967-7

Contact andyrudall@gmail.com
www.neatlittlerows.com

Printed in the United Kingdom

PREFACE

'It is my Royal and Imperial command that you exterminate the treacherous English and march over General French's contemptible little army.'

Kaiser Wilhelm II, 1914

'Very successful attack this morning... All went like clockwork... The battle is going very well for us and already the Germans are surrendering freely. The enemy is so short of men that he is collecting them from all parts of the line. Our troops are in wonderful spirits and full of confidence.'

Field Marshall Douglas Haig 1st July 1916

(Reported on the first day of an attack on The Somme, The British Army lost 20,000 men that day, most of them in the first hour of battle)

'I've seen devils coming up from the ground...I've seen hell upon this earth.'

Harry Patch 2005

'Gentlemen, our long wait is nearly at an end. Tomorrow morning, General Insanity Melchett invites you to a mass slaughter. We're going over the top.'

Captain Edmund Blackadder, 1989

SPECIAL THANKS

TO MY FAMILY

Nan, Mom, Dad and Lisa

Elaine, Mitchell and Tyler, Wendy, Dave and Ellis

TO MY LONGTIME FRIENDS AND NEW FRIENDS DISCOVERED DURING THE WRITING AND PUBLISHING OF THIS WORK

Chas & Jane Chambers, Ronald Harbach, Peter Clay, Ed Walker, Rob & Jackie Stokes, Ann & Tim Probyn, Dr H J Krijnen, Carine Declercq at Main Street Hotel Ypres, Dan Treby, Lorna Gavin, Jayne Heathcock, Jon Clay, Steve Goddard, Matthew May, Rosemary J Kind, Pierre Vandervelden, Lauren Edwards, The BBC 'Who Do You Think You Are' Team, Chris Moyles, Sue Jones, Spencer & Debbie Clay, Lieutenant Colonel C J E Seymour LVO, The Guards Museum London, The Great War Forum, The Commonwealth War Graves Commission, The Royal British Legion Poppy Appeal, Help For Heroes.

In remembrance of Guardsman Daniel Probyn (1984 – 2007).

To Grenadier Guards, past, present and future.

ACKNOWLEDGEMENTS

Grateful acknowledgement is made to the following for permission to quote and print material;

Excerpt from the '1st Battalion Grenadier Guards war diary for December 1914' courtesy of The National Archives.

Excerpt from 'For the Fallen' by Laurence Binyon.

Photographs of Daniel Probyn - Tim and Ann Probyn.

Photograph of Frederick John Dean – Steve Goddard.

Photograph of Richard John Dyer – Matthew May.

With appreciation and thanks to Olive Hackett (nee Cook), Harry's widow, (now deceased), for keeping the letters used in this book. Also to Dorothy (wife of Harry Hackett son of Harry) of Fowey for giving permission to use the material. To Jane Chambers (nee Hackett) and her sisters Carol and Ruth (granddaughters of Harry). And finally to Chas Chambers for his assistance in deciphering the hand-written letters.

INTRODUCTION

This book is based on facts as far as I am aware. I'm no World War One historian or expert by any stretch of the imagination. What I know about the war is simply what I've come across through my own research and experience. All the words, thoughts, feelings and understandings are entirely my own. I make no apologies for any errors however I do apologise for spelling, typos, grammar and the occasional lapse into 'Andy-speak'.

Neat Little Rows is essentially a book of two very distinct halves. Andy's Story is entirely my own journey of discovery and of 'Finding Harry'. It starts with an inconsequential, quite-by-chance event that happened to get me 'interested in the First World War' and ends with a visit to a physical landmark set in the quiet fields of Northern France. Harry's Story simply chronicles what I have pieced together of Harry Hackett's life and times. It is also seasoned with actual excerpts from some of the many letters written by Harry and sent to the love of his life, Olive. These letters have been carefully stored and have survived for almost a century.

Having been privileged to have been able to read every single letter and postcard, it has allowed me to obtain a glimpse of Harry's character. His words are humble, caring, unpretentious and entirely full of love for his sweetheart, Olive. In my opinion they are priceless and precious. In this day and age it's unusual for anyone to write 'love letters' anymore. Modern technology has put pay to this by offering us 'diluted', immediate text and email. Fortunately for us, we have access to Harry's innermost thoughts and feeling as they are embodied in the hand-written, neatly constructed pencil and ink communications.

Harry's Story also attempts to offer a 'dummies guide' to the 'war to end all wars' which Harry fought in. I hope, that although the two stories are essentially separated by around a hundred years, they offer a view on two people's lives that you will find interesting and maybe even a little enlightening.

Writing this book has affected my life in many different ways. I now know the streets of the Belgian city of Ypres like they were the back of my hand. I have had conversations with several World War One specialists and scholars. I've read and studied 'tons' of books, attended seminars and I've even completed the London Marathon in aid of Help for Heroes and in honour of Harry Hackett. I've met two of Harry's three granddaughters and have been in contact with the families of two of the soldiers Harry is buried next to. I've also become good friends with the proud parents of a modern day Grenadier who shares many similarities with our Harry.

So, why did I write this book?

I had better start by telling you that my brain is 'a little selective'. It doesn't allow me to store everything I see and do, including certain things I really, really want to remember. Some things just 'pass right through', yet other things that I might even consider unworthy of 'brain-RAM' stick in there. I can't tell you how many times Jacqui my wife reminds me of things we've done that I have absolutely no recall of. It's a little scary. So during the 'Finding of Harry' I decided to make notes in order to thwart my wayward grey matter.

Before I wrote this story the only thing I'd ever written of any worth before was an essay at school. It was at the Dingle Middle School, Kingswinford, in 1971 when I would have been about nine years old. The whole class was asked to 'write a piece' describing what they'd do to an ugly area of waste land next to a large concrete water tower near to our school. I remember coming up with an idea based around having all your shopping and leisure needs located in one place called something like 'Andy-Land'. I accompanied my essay with a detailed, coloured-in map-like drawing that included a huge supermarket, a sportswear store, a cinema and for some reason an ice-skating rink. The essays were judged by someone who my brain won't allow me to remember but who wasn't a teacher and I won! During one of the school assemblies this was announced and I remember being presented with, what appeared to me as, 'the smallest book in the world'. It was 'An Observer's Book of Nature'. Inside it was inscribed, by the presenter, with the details of my 'wondrous achievement'. It should be noted that up until that point I'd never even heard the words 'Shopping Mall', the concept, to me, just didn't exist. However, fourteen years after my 'prophetic-masterpiece', a facility known to one and all as The Merry Hill Centre opened about two miles away from 'Andy-Land'. It's the largest shopping centre in the area and has a huge supermarket or two, several sportswear stores, a multi-screen cinema but as yet no ice-rink!

"At school I was so rubbish at English that in my O-level English Literature exam I actually got a U for unclassified as my effort was so useless. So, who would have ever thought I'd be capable of writing a book? Never say never."

Andrew Mark Rudall, 2012

To my wife Jacqui for her constant love, friendship, patience and support.

To my kids Adison and Holli. This is your book to pass on.

In memory of my hero Sergeant Harry Hackett

And

The Fallen of the Great War

Andrew Mark Rudall – April 2012

TABLE OF CONTENTS

PREFACE 3

SPECIAL THANKS 4

ACKNOWLEDGEMENTS 5

INTRODUCTION 6

ANDY'S STORY 15

THE FREE BOOK 15
THE BACK TO SCHOOL BIT 16
THE TOE IN THE WATER 18
THE CHRIS MOYLES PODCAST 19
THE FIRST MENTION 20
THE NAN-TERNET 21
THE GENIUS-OLOGIST 22
THE CONFESSION 24
THE FINDING 25
THE VERY INTERESTING BIT 27
THE FAMILY CONTACT 28
THE COLONEL 29
THE TELLING 30
NEXT STOP FRANCE 31
THE PLACE OF PEACE 32
THE BIT AT THE END 34

HARRY'S STORY 48

EVERY END HAS A START 48
EVERY YOUNG LAD DREAMS OF BEING A SOLDIER 52
THE LETTERS 58
LIGHT THE BLUE TOUCH-PAPER AND RETIRE A SAFE DISTANCE 61
EVERY SOLDIER YEARNS FOR A BIT OF REAL ACTION...DON'T THEY? 63
JUST POPPING OFF TO WAR, I'LL BE BACK BY CHRISTMAS 68
SO WHAT OF THIS 'SALIENT' POINT? 71
SNIPER 1 – CLOTH CAP 0 73
ALL ABOUT YPRES 76
WELCOME TO MY HUMBLE ABODE 78
THE WESTERN FRONT...WAS IT EVER QUIET? 80

CHRISTMAS, THE SEASON OF GOODWILL AND PEACE. YEAH, RIGHT 83
IT WAS OK FOR THOSE BACK IN BLIGHTY...WASN'T IT? 88
SAMUEL HACKETT – HARRY'S LITTLE BROTHER 92
BACK TO OUR HARRY 97
SOME 'HUGE ASS' BATTLE IN THE SOMME 103
WHEN THE GOING GETS TOUGH, YOU NEED MORE TOUGHIES 107
NO SURRENDER, NO RUNNING AWAY, WE'RE BRITISH! 109
FIST VERSUS BULLET - DEATH MATCH 110
ONE DAY IN LE-TIR-ANGLAIS 113
REST IN PEACE HARRY WITH AN H.. 117
WE SHALL BE HEROES 118
DON'T FORGET TO REMEMBER THE FALLEN 119
POPPY POWER 121
SO IS IT TRUE WHEN THEY SAY, THE SHOW MUST GO ON? 122
AN UNCOMPLICATED HOPE 127

EPILOGUE 129

FACTS AND FIGURES 135

THE BROTHERS IN ARMS 136

MEMORIAL CASE AND MEDALS 141

SOME OF 'THE LETTERS' 143

THE WAR MEMORIAL... 147

PLACES AND POPPIES 148

BLACK COUNTRY TRANSLATIONS 150

GUARDSMAN DANIEL PROBYN............................... 156

ABOUT THE AUTHOR 158

FURTHER INFORMATION SOURCES 159

WHY...? 160

'Well, I ope it meks moowa sense than it 'ud ter a blind mon on a gollopin' hoss'

A Black Country saying for when you hope what you are trying to explain is understood correctly

ANDY'S STORY

The free book

In March 2009 I happened to buy a second-hand book by one of my favourite authors from a local charity shop in Stourbridge High Street. I'd been in the shop for no other reason than that I'd spotted a few hardbacks in 'neat little rows' in a window display. The thought crossed my mind that I could do with something a little different to read as, for one reason or another, I'd been consuming stacks of mountaineering and climbing books by the boat-load over the past few years. I'd 'done Everest and the Eiger to death' and just needed a break from frost-bite, crampons and bivouacs at 10,000 feet. After taking the book I'd chosen to the counter, the shop assistant told me it was 'buy one get one free' day and that I could select another book free of charge.

I'd already browsed through what they had to offer and didn't really see anything else I wanted, however, the fact that it was free persuaded me to look again. Being a little pushed for time I, quite literally, grabbed the nearest book to me. After a quick scan of the cover I thought 'that'll do' and took it to the counter.

A few weeks later I'd finished the book I'd originally picked out and was a bit stuck for reading material. So a little reluctantly I thought I'd give the 'free book' a whirl. I read the back cover review, flicked through it to see if there were any pictures and thought, 'I'll just read the first couple of pages'…surprisingly, I got into it. The overall story was not bad but it was the subject matter that really grabbed my attention. After only a few chapters I had developed a brand new 'interest'. This 'BOGOF' second-hand charity book is the reason you are reading these words.

The story was set in the 1914 to 1918 world war and mentioned a place known as The Ypres Salient. I'd never heard the word 'salient' before, but the book, albeit a historic fictional thriller, was so graphic and engaging that I was gripped. The horrors, gruesome goings-on and sacrifice of the blokes who were involved in this war known as 'The Great War', intrigued me. A 'salient' in simple terms for now, by the way, is a battlefield word for where the front fighting line juts out, in a U-shape, into enemy territory.

I imagine that most of us will have some notion of the First World War and how it changed things forever. Soldiers who'd enlisted in the army as a career prior to the start of the conflict were known as Regulars and couldn't possibly have had any idea of how horrendous it was going to be or what they would be expected to do. Following the outbreak of war and their initial choice to sign up, all the 'choosing' from then on would be done for them by officers whose main objective was to attempt to satisfy the insatiable appetite of an unstoppable, industrial war machine. As you probably know this would include ordering men to 'go over the top' and advance into the snaking horizontal spray of German machine guns that could, quite literally, cut a man in half.

Whenever I'd come across 'over the top' moments portrayed in films or on TV I'd often try to put myself in their boots and ask myself 'could I have done that?' I don't need to tell you what my answer would be, do I?

The back to school bit

Since the book I'd read was a made-up story set in this war, I thought it would be worth double-checking to see if what I'd read wasn't stretching the truth a little. Especially concerning the mud, blood, death, lice, gas, mutilation and general unpleasantness of trench warfare. So I thought it was time to start doing a little digging. After 'Googling' WW1 and doing some general research including trying to get my head around what a salient was, I eventually found myself on

Wikipedia and noticed a list of recommended books to read. I hopped across to Amazon and three days later a couple of books turned up in the patented brown Amazon cardboard wrapper. I'd bought 'The First Day on the Somme' and 'Somme 1916', simply because they were top of the recommended list and I'd also driven through an area signposted as 'The Somme' many times on my way to my wife Jacqui's sister's house in the Loire Valley and thought it'd be interesting to find out more about it. Also, and probably more interestingly, I remembered that The Somme was some kind of 'WW1 big deal' and it played an important part in my education as a young lad at the Dingle Primary School in Kingswinford.

Mr Williams, our teacher, had spent some time trying to educate us about WW1. At one point I specifically remember being asked to hold a great big fat black permanent marker pen and mark out something called 'The Western Front' on a huge colour map of some far-off place called Europe. Bearing in mind I'd be about nine at the time, this task was a huge responsibility in my eyes. Firstly, I had one chance to get this right, permanent markers are permanent. Secondly, all the other kids were miffed that they hadn't been chosen to wield the pen of permanency. Thirdly, my mom would have a paddy if I got any ink on my white school shirt. To my amazement 'the big black line' was spot on and the map took centre stage on the main wall in our classroom. Over the next few weeks we proceeded to add pins with string attached to notes and pictures as Mr Williams began to explain some key 'Great War' events to us.

The 'pièce de résistance' for us as kids was that as part of our studies our class was taken on a school trip to the Imperial War Museum in London. I remember seeing odd-shaped tanks, rockets, medals and planes made out of what looked like newspaper and string. All this was quite a while ago now but of all my childhood learning experiences I think the whole WW1 stuff really must've hit a prime bit of brain real estate. I mention this because one day in April of 2009 I happened to return to the very same museum, quite by chance, with Jacqui, as we were in the area and had a couple of hours to kill. At the museum tons of memories started flooding back. Words like 'Ferdinand', 'British Expeditionary Force (B.E.F.)', 'Whizz-bang' and 'Kaiser' sparked off distant memories as my brain 'Googled' itself. It's about now that you're probably thinking 'he's rambling a bit' so I'll get back to my tale.

The toe in the water

Now that I had a little 'Somme' knowledge from the books I'd read, I decided that next time I drove through the area in France I'd head off the autoroute and point my sat-nav at a town that was in the middle of it, called Albert. We did this in May of the same year and ended up at a place called Beaumont Hamel and the beautiful (if that's an appropriate word for a place where thousands of men died) Newfoundland Memorial Park. My daughter Holli lost interest after 90 seconds and sneaked back to the car to resume Facebooking and texting, teenagers, eh? It's sad to think that most of the lads who died at Beaumont Hamel would have been around her age. How times change! Jacqui and I carried on and had a private whistle-stop tour escorted by a superbly knowledgeable Canadian tour guide. Actually being there, seeing the battlefield, meant we got a general idea of the reality of trench warfare. As we were leaving I picked up a stone from one of the trenches and slipped it in my pocket ... don't ask, it's just something I do. We returned home a few days later and I read more and more war books.

In July, Jacqui and I decided to visit a city that had a massive link with WW1. It was known as Ypres or Ieper but referred to by our troops as 'Wipers'. Here, after visiting the Menin Gate and Tyne Cot Cemetery, I was conscious that some 'tourists' laying wreaths, bright red poppies and tiny wooden crosses obviously had relatives who had been involved and perhaps fought and died in this area. I wondered what they must be thinking and feeling being in the spot where their relatives had perished. I held that thought....

After a couple of days in Ypres, we headed back towards the autoroute after a quick trip to a very unusual museum at Sanctuary Wood run by a huge round man with poorly feet whose toenails looked like pork scratchings. On our journey we drove through a place called Bailleul then on to St Omer on our way to spend our summer holiday in the Loire. Along the quiet country roads I remember pointing out a surprising number of British cemeteries enclosing large white crosses. At a particular set of traffic lights, for no apparent reason we both noticed a car parked up that had been abandoned so long there was grass growing on the inside of it and next to it a house with a very peculiarly designed 'lightning-bolt' adorned front door that looked like a superhero must live there ... strange what you notice sometimes.

The Chris Moyles podcast

After two week's holiday I left Jacqui with her sister Elaine as she was going to help out with some painting and decorating and I returned home to get back to work. The plan was that I'd return after a couple of weeks to pick Jacqui up and drop off my daughter Holli as she wanted a week away with her auntie Elaine and cousin Tyler. It was while I was driving home from the Channel Tunnel on the M20 that I happened to listen to a Chris Moyles radio show podcast. Chris is a DJ on Radio 1 and he was talking with his team about the fact that he'd recently appeared on an episode of a BBC 'Who Do You Think You Are?' programme. It sounded mildly interesting, but I thought no more of it.

A few days later there was nothing on telly so I was browsing BBC's iPlayer online and noticed a web link advertising the very same episode. I watched it and have to admit I whizzed it on a few minutes at the start until I noticed a shot of the unique and impressive Grote Markt building in the centre of Ypres where Jacqui and I had recently visited. The programme then focussed on Chris's great-grandad James Moyles, who had served in the British Army somewhere near Ypres. It showed Chris driving through the city and this got my attention primarily because I recognised some of the streets, shops and buildings.

Near the end of the programme Chris was very clearly taken aback when the 'WDYTYA' guide took him to more or less the spot where his relative had been killed in action in 1914. It was pretty touching stuff. The final shot framed Chris leaning on the bonnet of a 4x4 looking at a newspaper account of his great-grandad's death, then turning his head pensively to view what looked like a 'potato' field where it had all happened. Watching this prompted a terrible thought in me. I was...and you'll have to forgive me for this...a bit jealous.

Let me explain: It was basically that someone, i.e. Chris, had a blood relative who was a hero and had served and died in 'The Salient', 'Wipers', 'The First World War'. Chris's great-grandad had experienced the horror, noise, smells, pain and fear and had been in the midst of 'The Great War'. I've no idea why I had this 'jealous' thought, but I just did. You can't help these things sometimes, can you? After the programme it sparked a question that I was sure I knew the answer to and that answer was 'No, Andrew Rudall, I'm afraid you don't have any blood relatives who served or died in World War 1 or any war for that matter'.

But I thought, it wouldn't hurt to double-check, would it?

The first mention

Where to start? I phoned my mom and dad and after a little bit of brain racking mom said, 'Well, come to think of it, I seem to vaguely remember your nan mentioning some uncle or cousin or somebody in the family who'd died in the First World War'. My ears pricked up like Wile E Coyote's would if he'd just heard the distant 'meep-meep' of a roadrunner. There was a glimmer of hope! Then mom said, 'She said he was in some regiment with something to do with the Grenadier Guards'. The glimmer turned to gloom: how could I possibly have a relative in the Grenadier Guards? Let's face it a Black Country lad in the elite Regiment of Grenadier Guards! So I totally discounted it. Mom said she thought his name was Harry Hackett. I started searching and hit the Commonwealth War Graves site first not expecting to find anyone. I thought Hackett wasn't a very common name. At first look there were thirteen! I studied every single one of them.

I was looking for any information that would link a Harry or even a Harold Hackett with the Black Country, my local area. Not too long after, I found someone whom I thought was a strong contender. There was a Harold Hackett, believe it or not, from Hackett Street, Blackheath. Blackheath is right next to where my nan's family, the Hacketts, used to live and I was pretty sure I'd found our man. It also stated that he'd been in the Royal Warwickshire Regiment which made sense as I reckoned blokes from 'round here' would probably have been recruited into the Staffordshire, Worcestershire or Warwickshire regiments. I had a name, service number, date of death and location of a grave. Of all of this information the grave site really pressed a few buttons for me. It took a little while to take this in as I realised I might be able to visit an actual relative's grave like the thousands I'd already seen during my travels to Ypres and The Somme.

At this point my mind started to buzz due to the realisation that there was a very strong possibility I actually have had a relative associated with the Great War! I didn't let myself get too over excited as I was still only 90% sure it was Harry. I needed the additional 10%. Without it I just wouldn't be able to fully commit myself or immerse myself in the full implications of this evidence. I decided to check it out and popped around to my nan's place to run it past her.

The Nan-ternet

My nan, Annie Nock, who was 96 at the time, was pretty switched on with facts and figures but I had a problem with what my mom had said nan had remembered. The link with the Grenadier Guards couldn't be true…could it? It just sounded way off the mark and totally improbable. I had to explain to her how I'd found the information I was about to run past her, which meant I had to mention the 'internet' word. This made my nan raise an eyebrow as I suppose at 96 the thought of being able to find information so quickly while sitting in your front room using a wireless laptop is all a little bit like spooky voodoo. She listened and I mentioned how the Warwickshire Regiment was more likely to be where Harry joined up rather than the Grenadiers. But as soon as I mentioned that the Harry I'd found lived in Hackett Street, Blackheath she shook her head and said with absolute crystal clear authority "It's not him. Harry lived at 46, High Street, Old Hill with his brothers Thomas, Levi, George, Joe and Sam. There is no way he lived in Hackett Street because I know Hackett Street as there was a murder there". Murder, eh? Now that's a whole other story and nothing at all to do with my family, I might add. She also re-iterated that he was definitely in 'the Grenadiers' and that he was stationed somewhere in London where he met his wife Olive, who had moved there from Fowey in Cornwall to work in the 'posh' Pimlico suburbs as a domestic servant.

I was, to say the least, disappointed by my research. What I thought were the entire resources of the internet had been thwarted by a 96 year old lady sitting in her big chair in front of her ancient TV next to her 'holy writings' also known as 'The TV Choice' magazine. That said, nan is pretty good with remembering 'old things' and the fact she'd remembered the street and house number proved to me that the Harold I'd found on the war graves site, from Blackheath, wasn't the Harry I was looking for.

Returning home after chatting a little more about her dad, Thomas, who was Harry's older brother, and the other five brothers who 'were all very tall men', I decided to look at the list of thirteen once more. I must admit I did notice an 'H. Hackett' who was in the Grenadier Guards in the list before, but totally discounted it as it was 'H' not a 'Harry' or 'Harold'. There was absolutely no further information like where he lived and there were no relatives shown as most of the others in the list had. So, bearing in mind what my nan had said, this chap listed as 'H. Hackett' of the Grenadier Guards 'could' possibly be our relative, I supposed. However I had nothing to substantiate it.

I was back, not quite to square one, but more like square one and a half. The half being the fact that if nan had remembered correctly there was at least something to go on.

The Genius-ologist

After a few days of letting everyone else use Google, without it being hogged by me running searches mostly made up of H, Harry, Hackett, Old Hill, Grenadier Guards, WW1, I thought I might need some specialist help in my quest. After asking a few folks I work with if they knew anyone who 'did genealogy stuff' they immediately responded with, 'ask Sue Jones in finance, she's an expert, it's her thing'. Within three seconds of hearing this I was on the phone speaking to Sue seeking her advice. She asked for a couple of general family names and dates and said the best thing to do would be to get as many birth, death and marriage certificates as I could. We arranged to meet one lunchtime to see what we could find out online.

That night I scooted around to my mom and dad's to see what info they might have. I left with tons of birth, death and marriage certificates and stuff that I never even knew existed before. I reckoned Sue would be most impressed. We met and immediately, using her skills on the Ancestry.co.uk website, all sorts of family info was popping up on screen. It was mind blowing! Nevertheless, I desperately wanted to see if I could locate any information to find Harry Hackett and, more to the point, see if I could link any of that information to any of the thirteen Harrys. Sue explained that ancient census information could be a little erroneous. Christian names on birth certificates may not be the same as those 'given on the doorstep' to the censor. For example, my great-grandmother Hagar is listed as Aggie on one census form. Likewise there may just be simple spelling mistakes which are probably due to the hand-writing in the early 1900's. However, with Sue's help, after a little detective work we found my great-great-grandparents on the 1911 census and, sure enough, Harry Hackett was there listed next to his father, mother and nine siblings.

This was the first bit of hard evidence I'd seen other than what nan had said and it indicated his age and occupation along with those of everyone else in the house at the time. From this Sue was able to work out his approximate date of birth and finally we found a military record for one Harry Hackett of the Grenadier Guards listed as being born in Old Hall, Dudley (note 'Old Hall' not 'Old Hill'). I had totally missed this detail as 'Old Hall' isn't 'Old Hill' and Old Hill isn't in Dudley, it's in Staffordshire. Sue's experience came in to play here as she explained that 'Old Hill' could have easily been written down as 'Old Hall' 'back then' and that little 'typos' like this were part and parcel of researching old records.

I was reasonably chuffed as this new military information confirmed his service record number, regiment and battalion. I was really grateful to Sue. Without her help there is no way I'd have been able to get as far as I did.

Later on that evening, on the internet, I'd pretty quickly found H. Hackett's grave location on the Commonwealth Graves Commission website. But (and this was a big mother of a but) I was not 100% sure this was my great-grandad's brother. I guess it was because the address stating Old Hall, Dudley may not have been a typo and could quite possibly mean I'd found the wrong Harry Hackett. Also the fact that he was listed as a Grenadier Guard still just didn't sound right; a Black Country lad in the London based Grenadier Guards? So, after getting this close I still wasn't convinced and didn't tell any of my family anything about what I'd discovered. I thought it would be a bit bonkers to share this info and then find out that it was some other soldier who simply happened to have the same name.

Within seven days of starting my search for a 'soldier' I was really close to knowing, but not absolutely sure, I'd found him. Without 100% surety I wouldn't believe it. I'm pretty sure I know what faith is but I didn't have enough faith to put my trust in a typo. Having a 'relative' who served and died in the Great War would be too important for me to base on a probability. I simply had to know it for a fact. I don't know why but, to me, it was absolutely vital that I knew without a doubt before I stepped over the line from 'possibly him' to 'definitely him'.

Now I guess you may be thinking here 'Whoa! hold on a minute, what's he on about here? line? what line?' Well, in my opinion (and I stress my opinion), having a blood relative connecting my life to such a major episode in our world history is more than a little important to me.

It's serious personal stuff and really hard to explain in words. But then again I suppose it wouldn't hurt to try, so here goes.

The confession

I......collect......rocks. Yes, you heard right. I collect rocks from all sorts of places around the world. If I'm at a place that I like, or is significant, I pick up a fifty pence-sized stone, rock, brick or pebble and stick it in my pocket. I don't do it everywhere I go, but now and again I do collect the odd rock especially from locations where big things have happened such as a historic site, building, battlefield, beach or landmark. The only reason, I think, that I do this is that the little piece of 'our planet' in some weird way allows me to connect to that place or event in a 'this little rock was actually there when x, y or z happened' kind of way. I suppose it's a bit like collecting a 3D physical autograph that you can hold in your hand and touch and smell even. Now I know this may make you think I'm a little 'special' but not in a 'he has a special gift kind of way' but, hey, 'each to his own'. Anyway, what of lines and rocks? The link is simply The Great War via a direct relative to me. 'Crossing the line' as I put it would be 'knowing this as a fact' and rather than a rock in my hand connecting me indirectly to an event that it had been near to in history, I'd be linked by blood.

(Note if you can follow any of this we need to talk as we'd probably make good 'wavelength friends').

So let's recap. I have found a Harry Hackett (big tick), in the Grenadier Guards (big tick) who was from Old Hall that might or might not be Old Hill (tiny tick). So what was I going to do about this tiny tick? Or more to the point what could I possibly do in order to get three big ticks? I'd had a seriously clever genealogist enthusiast-type person help me find the info so far, so how could I take the information I had and get it from 'pretty sure that's him' to 'this person is 100% bona fide the Harry Hackett from 46, High Street, Old Hill?'

The finding

I had no bright ideas how to do this so, while Jacqui was still away on holiday, I just spent hours and hours 'Googling like a nutter'. I tried a zillion searches using all the keywords I could muster. After finding nothing I just started browsing through pages and pages of 'Grenadier Guard-type' sites. Finally, in the early hours of one morning, after quite a while staring at my laptop screen, I found something very, very, very interesting.

It was a Grenadiers' modest-looking website listing information about the Officers and Enlisted Men of WW1. I clicked on the Enlisted Men link and at first couldn't find a single Hackett. Looking closer, there at the bottom of the main page and not particularly easy to see at first glance, was a link to an alphabetical listing of enlisted men by surname. I couldn't move the mouse quickly enough. In my haste I scrolled past the 'H' at least three times. I finally clicked on it and waited while what looked like a large PDF document started to load. I hoped it wouldn't tell me what I already knew which was basically name, initial, service number, rank, battalion, casualty, place died, date died, age and place of rest. The document loaded and it was a table showing exactly the items I'd expected for everyone with a name starting with the letter 'H'. I also noticed it had an additional remarks column which was generally blank.

I hit the page-down key expecting to have to browse through hundreds of names again and it started to scroll through name after name. Then, up popped a couple of photos within the body of the table. I stopped and thought it might be interesting to see what the pictures showed. At first I could see three pictures side by side; a chap with a woman in a typical 'me and the missus' WW1 soldier pose, then a couple of soldier 'team-type' group photos. I was about to scroll on when I noticed the line above the pictures. It read 'HACKETT'.

In fact it read, name 'HACKETT' followed by the initial 'H', service number '15331', rank 'SERGEANT'. As I was aware of all this information already I thought, 'Oh good, I've spotted the Harry Hackett that might or might not be my relative'.

Then I spotted something 'heart-stopping' that 'changed things'.

Under the remarks column was the following, crucial, information I'd been searching for: 'Married to Olive Hackett of, (wait for it)…46, High Street, Old Hill, Staffordshire'. Heart-rate well on the rise here; I thought, 'Wow! just like nan told me'. The address and name of Harry's wife was 100% spot on. I was gob smacked!! Now, bear in mind, Jacqui was away in France. I hadn't told any of the family about my quest. I had no one to tell. I was 'home alone'. It was really late. I couldn't call anyone. I was 'buzzing' and thought that my search had come to an end. Harry Hackett 15331 was my blood relative…but it didn't end there.

After a few moments with myself letting this sink in and jumping around the bedroom like a gibbon who had just won a 'free bananas for life' competition, I returned to looking at the photos, not thinking they were related in any way. However the text beneath them read 'Harry Hackett (15331) pictured top left with other unknown Grenadier Guards'. The pictures were all of Harry!!! The 'me and the missus' photo was Harry seated next to his wife Olive. My 'expectation-o-meter' had already been blown through the roof by finding out Harry was my relative but having the pictures as well just took the experience to a whole new level.

I was staring in to the eyes of Harry in his uniform with his Sergeant stripes clearly on his left arm. For a split second I also had a very strange feeling because his face reminded me of ... me. It's hard to explain seeing someone who resembles you to anyone who hasn't experienced it and it was, shall we say, 'most odd'.

So after a few calming breaths accompanied by a few long stares at the ceiling I thought "I'm there, I have confirmation and photos". I can't wait to tell my family as they, like me, will be blown away and to say the least unbelievably proud. I, too, like Chris Moyles and all those folks laying wreaths and crosses at Ypres now had a bona fide Great War connection. After book-marking the web page containing the photos I was about to logout and shutdown as it was so late but for some reason I just happened to hit the page-down key again out of curiosity.

The next couple of images weren't more photographs but a colour map that I recognised as being the Ypres Salient and next to it a scanned image of a really, really old postcard.

The very interesting bit

The postcard was from Harry to Olive. I deciphered the hand-written words very carefully, they read;

> Dear O, I am sending you this postcard with two of the
> German soldiers addresses on, which I got on Boxing Day.
> I suppose you saw in the papers about us going across, out
> of the trenches and having a word or two together. Hope
> you are well as it leaves me at present.
> With Love, from Harry.

I read it again, then again, blinked, rubbed my eyes, squinted, then read it once again. I let out a slow, perfectly-formed sentence of fabulously explicit language befitting the moment. I sat back on my chair, took a deep breath, covered my mouth with my hand and read it again. I then said "******* hellfire, he was at 'The Christmas Truce!!'", 'He was there', 'Oh my life!'

Let's say, I was ever so pleased.

I didn't sleep that night.

Another recap. Seven days before I hadn't even known for sure that Harry had existed. Then I found he was a relative who had served and died for his country in WW1 with the Grenadier Guards. And now, astonishingly, I had discovered he was part of one of the most unusual, unscripted acts of humanity now known as 'The Christmas Truce 1914'.

The family contact

I immediately emailed the person listed as the webmaster of the Guards site I'd found this information. I asked if he had any contact details for the Chambers family who, I'd spotted were, listed as providing the original photos and postcard. Within a few hours I'd received an email acknowledging my request with a message saying that he would try but the last contact was some time ago, meaning this was unlikely. I expected the trail to go cold but later that very same day I received an email from Chas Chambers who must've wondered what I was up to. I replied with a list of names and details showing how I was related to Sergeant Harry Hackett. He responded, now knowing I wasn't some mad stalker, and explained that Harry and Olive had a son (also known as Harry) who'd lived in Cornwall. Chas also added that he was married to Jane who is one of Sergeant Harry's three grand-daughters. I quickly asked if Harry junior was anything to do with the Post Office. He confirmed that 'yes' he had worked for them. I then explained that I asked because when I was really young, possibly around ten years old, I'd been taken by Dan and Annie Nock (my nan and grandad) to visit a relative called Harry, who was 'well up in the Post Office', at his bungalow on a hill in Cornwall. This would have been Harry junior. Bear with me, I know it's confusing having two Harrys.

I remembered the visit vividly and remembered sitting in his front garden, watching a train go by in the distance. Chas and I then emailed each other over the next few days with snippets of information, family tree diagrams and general family 'gossip'. It was great to experience contact with a distant relative who had a similar interest in family history. His 'genealogy' skills and advice were really helpful to me and filled in quite a few blanks. Now that I had the hard evidence and the 100% surety I'd been looking for I started to collate all my information as I'd soon need to share it with my family and let them in on the secret. Before that I did a little more research just to try and add as much detail as possible. It was also time I made contact with the Grenadier Guards.

The Colonel

It didn't take much effort to find the official 'Grenadier Guards' Museum' website. The site had a family research page and I was on the phone to them the next day. They explained that they offered a service whereby they would search for a Grenadiers' records, make a copy and send them to you for a small fee. I posted my cheque about three seconds after I'd put the phone down.

About a week later at work I had a call put through to me by my colleague Lauren. She spun around on her chair, covered the mouthpiece, raised both eyebrows, made an 'I think I'm being wound-up face' and mouthed the words 'Colonel Seymour...something about a soldier...for you?' I took the call and was greeted by what I can only explain as an extremely posh army bloke. He spoke just like you'd expect a Colonel in the Grenadiers to speak, that is to say a full, rich Queen's English voice laced with authority and lashings of character. He explained in his fantastic 'General Melchett of Blackadder Goes Forth-like' voice that he had found some information on Harry and that he'd post it to me as soon as he could. However, a few of his archivists were on holiday so it would take a while as it was 'absolute chaos here at the moment'. Even though the Colonel had, to me, a scary commanding headmaster-like way about him, he made me feel very much at ease and we had a good few minutes rattling on about Harry, the Battle of the Lys and army field ambulances, would you believe? While I had him on the phone I felt I just had to ask 'How on earth could a lad from the Black Country end up in the 'London-based' Grenadiers?' Colonel Seymour said, 'That was perfectly usual as the West Midlands was and still is an important recruiting ground as it is the 'spine of England''.

It's probably worth stating here that 'the Colonel' is in fact none other than Lieutenant Conway Seymour LVO (Lieutenant of the Victorian Order) who was until recently the highest ranking Grenadier Guard based at Wellington Barracks, (the Guards headquarters), just across the way from Buckingham Palace!

After my quick chat with the Colonel I was enormously proud and felt a part of the whole Grenadier family. I know that sounds a little daft but it's how I felt. I think I sensed a certain bond with the history and the Colonel certainly encouraged this with his openness and appreciation for Harry's valiant contribution in the Great War. He even stated 'he was a hero'. Anyway, we said our goodbyes and I placed the handset slowly and precisely down. I then leaned back in my chair and slowly swivelled around towards Lauren, who was still looking agog at me following my 'old pals-type' chat with a real live Colonel. I looked her straight in the eye and said, with a cheeky grin, 'Do you have a war hero in your family?' She gave me her best (and not unusual) 'what is he on?' type look, shook her head and rolled her eyes to the ceiling. It's a look I know well.

The telling

Equipped with print-outs, scribbled notes, scraps of paper and emails I decided it was now time to share this information, that I'd been sitting on for seven days, with my family. So, as my beloved Jacqui was still in France, I set off on my motorbike to my mom and dad's. I ordered a strong coffee and the best seat in the house. Carefully I set out my portfolio of information and when they were settled I began. They were pretty amazed to hear what I had to tell them and I had to go over a few things a couple of times because it's a lot to take in at one go. One strange thing was that at one point when I showed my mom Harry's photograph, she said to my dad, "Oooh, Mal, he doesn't half look like our Andrew".

Next stop France

The weekend arrived and it was time to do my taxi duties and rescue Jacqui from her paintbrush and sandpaper and at the same time drop off Holli who'd arranged to spend a week in the sun. I'd then get a chance to tell the 'How I Found Harry' story to the rest of our family at Elaine and Mitchell's beautiful French home known as La Colline.

Driving through France this time on the way to them was a little strange as I knew Harry's grave was only about forty minutes away from Calais. I was really tempted to just drive to the war cemetery at Hazebrouck, but thought my priority was getting to Jacqui as I hadn't seen her for two weeks and Holli was desperate to work on her tan and read her stack of 'Hello' magazines while lying in the sun. Five hours after popping out of the Eurotunnel, we pulled up on the gravel-lined driveway of La Colline. That evening I got my paperwork and laptop ready for my presentation under the coloured bunting lights next to the pool with the sun just starting to set in the valley. David, Wendy, Ellis, Elaine, Tyler, Jacqui and Holli listened in silence. They were all spellbound. I noticed a few tears in eyes, and as I worked through surprise after surprise, I witnessed synchronised jaw dropping. Oh, yes, and I also got the 'He doesn't half look like you Andy' response a few times as well when I showed them a blown-up printed picture of Harry sitting next to Olive.

Although I never said it out loud, I was itching to visit Hazebrouck and find Harry's grave. Jacqui had been at La Colline for four weeks so I knew she'd want to get home pretty sharpish to see our beloved doggies Booi and Radley. I thought it best not to suggest a detour or impromptu visit. However, whilst walking one evening past a vast, golden sunflower field, generally chatting and catching up on the gossip, Jacqui said, 'How about we go home a little earlier and pop to see if we can find Harry?' She didn't have to ask me twice and we made plans to leave early next morning taking the route home via the outskirts of Paris then on towards the small town of Hazebrouck in Flanders, Northern France.

The place of peace

As we left the family and brought the car up to 'attack speed' (130kph) on the autoroute I started to feel a little anxious because in a few hours, all being well, I'd be standing next to my great-great uncle Harry Hackett's grave. It's hard to explain exactly what I was experiencing. I suppose I was sensing an 'inevitability' where the little clues and threads of information of the past two weeks would serve their purpose and deliver me to Hazebrouck, Cinq Rues Cemetery, row B, grave 7.

It sounds a bit strange, this, but at times it had felt like certain information had been searching for me rather than the other way around.

As we got closer, the more and more anxious and emotional I started to feel but 'as-you-do' I tried to keep a lid on it. I don't know if Jacqui noticed my little tell-tale 'I'm getting worried' signs. I think I also felt a little in awe of actually being physically close to Harry along with the fact that for the past couple of weeks he'd had a unique influence on my life. Also, there's the sadness of visiting a grave and, in Harry's case, the circumstances of his death.

Finally, we reckoned we were fifteen miles from Hazebrouck and Jacqui started to guide us by following a very simple map I'd printed out 'just in case' the sat-nav went all 'computer says no' on us. A few villages later at about 6:00pm on a beautiful summer evening we reached the 'centre-ville' and followed our noses until the road headed west towards St Omer. Not far out of town we spotted a large white stone cross on the right of the road surrounded by a little brick wall and a gate with 200 or so white grave stones.

I pulled the car off the road next to the gate and turned off the engine. We sat there in silence for a few seconds at first. I was just trying to take things in and contemplate what we were about to experience. There wasn't a soul about only the odd car and a few cows chewing away on grass in a nearby field. Jacqui jumped out and calmly started walking towards the identical headstones all in 'neat little rows'.

I waited by the gate wanting to remember everything I was seeing and feeling. I breathed deeply just trying to take it all in. Within a minute she waved me over and pointed to a single grave.

After preparing my thoughts and taking a deep breath I approached and found myself standing on a patch of very well groomed grass in front of a simple grey-white grave stone bearing the name H. Hackett. I'd memorised the other details on the stone after seeing them on screen or old bits of paper and by typing them into search engines hundreds of times.

I doffed my baseball cap and I just stood there for ages and ages next to Jacqui.........and Harry.

The bit at the end

Since writing down these thoughts, information and details have continued to come my way almost on a daily basis. It's amazing what I've learned and been able to share with family and friends. I cannot begin to tell you how proud I am to have had relative who must have seen, been through and experienced things none of us could ever begin to fully perceive or appreciate. That, along with being a Sergeant in the Grenadier Guards and getting married and having a son and fighting a war, is beyond me. The fact that I've read so many accounts of Great War battles has helped me to get an idea of what things may have been like, but as you know, the difference between reading a book compared to actually being there is, immeasurable.

I just can't imagine what Harry must have seen and done.

Oh, by the way, I have missed one little detail out of the story and I think it is worth a mention.

Do you remember near the start of this story when Jacqui and I were making our way back from Ypres and we noticed 'something strange' involving a car with grass inside it and a weird 'lightning-bolt' front door? Well, as we left Harry's grave we must've only driven a few hundred metres when Jacqui said, 'Do you know it's funny but I feel like we've been here before'. I agreed and said that it did seem a little familiar for some reason, even though French country roads can look a bit samey-samey. Jacqui said 'It reminds me of that place where we noticed that strange car with the grass on the inside and that house with the weird front door'. No sooner had the word 'door' left her lips but we pulled up at some traffic lights and across the way.........was the exact same car and the exact weird front door. This meant that only weeks before we'd passed through this exact spot and, of course, in doing so had passed a few metres from Harry's grave.

Back then we'd never even heard mention of his name or even known he had existed. Who'd have thought it, eh?

Harry, you will not be forgotten. I promise.

HARRY AND HIS WIFE OLIVE

HARRY HACKETT'S GRAVE IN CINQ RUES

GRAVE SITE CERTIFICATE TO INDICATE HARRY'S TEMPORARY GRAVE SITE

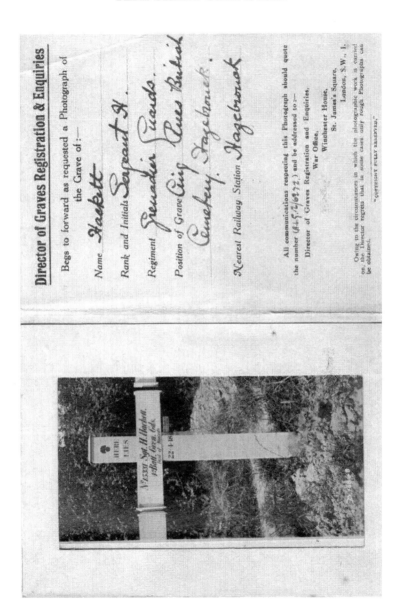

THE POSTCARD

THE ADDRESS SHOWS THE HOUSE WHERE OLIVE LIVED.
IT IS STILL THERE TODAY AND LOCATED IN LONDON W2

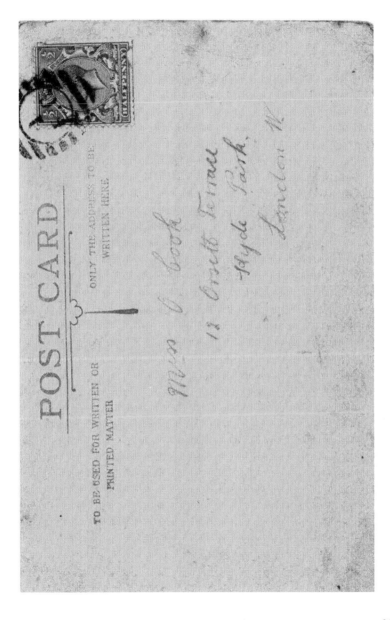

HARRY (LEFT) WITH SOLDIERS RECOVERING AT A
HOSPITAL IN DORSET. DATE UNKNOWN

THE FIRST TIME ANDY & JACQUI VISITED CINQ RUES CEMETERY NEAR HAZEBROUCK ON, 9TH AUGUST 2009

THE FIRST TIME ANDY MET HARRY

A WREATH AND A FEW MEMORIAL NOTES WE PLACED AT HARRY'S GRAVE IN OCTOBER 2009

Well, e's took 'is eggs to a fine market, ay 'e?

A Black Country saying for when someone who
showed great promise comes to an untimely end

'Joining up'

A short Black Country conversation

"Owbin ya me owd taerter?"

"Bay ter bad. Ars yerself chap?"

"Bostin, omma jiynen th'armay bay I"

"Yow, bay bin ya?"

"Ar bin, omma jiynen the Grenadiers an all"

"Well I be bloed. Ar bet tha fairthers chuffed aye e?"

"Ar. E sez I shaw bi no wuss off than I bin eya. An itul be ova afower Krismuss woe et?"

"Cors et ull, cocker. Any road I cor stop a cantin I best be gooin. Yo tek care mi mon an keep yer yed dowen"

"I sholl"

"Tararabit"

"Tarar chap"

HARRY'S STORY

Every end has a start

Harry Hackett was named Harry. Not Harold, just plain and simple Harry. He was a Black Country lad. His mom and dad were Samuel and Maria. They all lived in Old Hill at number 46, High Street. This street has long since been lost by the modernisation juggernaut that is relentless in its quest to deliver bigger and better roads. All, of course, brimming with the obligatory lashings of road signs and associated street furniture. A new, modern layout, has rubbed the Hackett home out as it muscled its way in, in the name of progress and change. However, a little bit of the road still remains, apparently in the form of Highgate Street. The house was home to Harry's mom and dad, his five brothers and four sisters. It's said that Harry was the apple of his mother's eye. I know, that as parents, you are not supposed to have favourites, but perhaps he just held a special place in her heart.

By means of background; Old Hill is a parish in the heart of the Black Country a couple of miles south of Dudley. From 1770 to 1970 this area was one of the largest centres in the country renowned for engineering excellence. It has also been described in years past as being 'the Workshop of the World'.

I can't recall any famous people, musicians or sportsmen, who hail from Old Hill. But I do know that it was one of a few villages in the area that was famous for chain and anchor making. It's also a location where many local women made a meagre living as chain makers in the late 1800's and early 1900's. My great-grandma Hagar (Aggie) Hackett was a Black Country chain maker around the turn of the century. Her chain-shop, or 'brew-house' as they called it, was in the back garden of their 'two-up two-down' house in Best Street, Old Hill. During the First World War the military required vast amounts of chain to equip the war-horses and associated wagons. This meant that anyone who could was required to make chain because there was plenty of work available. But it wasn't very well paid. My nan has often told me of the times she would have to 'mind' one of her younger sisters in the 'brew-house' while her mom pounded the glowing, red-hot metal into shape. She recalls the sparks and embers flying around and burning tiny holes in their clothes.

Near to where I live is the Black Country Living Museum at Dudley, West Midlands. It's an open-air museum with reconstructed buildings to walk through and explore. On the main street there are several terraced houses and shops all in a row. One of them is known as the 'chain-maker's house'. Nan always said that this house 'could've been the house we all lived in'. It's pretty much identical in layout and décor. Regarding what was the tiny back garden, which was really taken up by the outside loo and workshop, my grandad also once recalled, 'I remember when I was courting your nan, her mother used to call me out to the 'brew-house' to work the bellows for her so as to keep the coals nice and hot'. This was to save my great-grandma (and his future mother-in-law) a bit of effort while she continued to make chain well into the late evening.

People that live in the Black Country are very proud of the way they speak. Black Country people will all tell you emphatically that their accent must not under any circumstances be confused or classed as 'Brummie', the Birmingham accent. If you want to upset a 'Yam Yam', (a reference to a Black Country person's use of 'yow am' or yow'm instead of 'you are'), simply comment on their 'Brummie accent'. You will probably be met with something like, 'Ar bay a Brummie coz ar bisn't from Brummagem bin I?

Black Country is much more than just an accent, it has its own dialect and vocabulary. This dialect remains, perhaps, one of the last examples of early English still spoken today. It's quite common, and I say this from my own experience, that often people who 'speak the dialect' and have been educated locally will only speak the language when they are with family and friends or down the pub. When they are at work or speaking to people who aren't from the area they 'spake proper' and revert to standard English. There is a general feeling in the UK that dialects are 'dying out', a process referred to as dialect levelling. However, there is also evidence that distinct regional dialects including 'Black Country' are alive and kicking. You might also argue that some new modern-day dialects are actually emerging. For instance the hybrid called 'Jafaican' (fake Jamaican or to use it's official title, Multicultural London English) is probably more common than, say, the celebrated Cockney dialect. 'Safe, man. You lookin' buff in dem low batties. Dey's sick innit, man', would make perfect sense in many inner city areas.

A couple of miles from my great-grandma's house in Old Hill there was an established company called Noah Hingley of Netherton. They made most of the chains and the huge anchor for the famous White Star Line R.M.S. Titanic. When it was completed it took twenty shire-horses to transport the anchor alone from Netherton to the railway station in Dudley. There's a replica outside the Black Country Museum today, it's an absolute 'whopper'.

Harry, our Black Country lad, was born, on Saturday 3 January 1891. On this very day another 'titanic' Black Country event was taking place as Wolverhampton Wanderers were playing arch-rivals West Bromwich Albion in an English Football League fixture. This gargantuan local event is known as 'The Black Country Derby'. It's still hugely popular and an eagerly anticipated match each and every season. The banter between rival fans in schools, pubs, on Twitter and in local newspapers is priceless and a constant source of teasing, one-upmanship and point scoring. Wolves, fortunately or unfortunately, depending on loyalties, won 4 – 0. Some of you 'footie-buffs' out there may well appreciate the rivalry between Wolves (the Dingles) and Albion (the Baggies) and to some West Brom fans, losing 4 – 0 would have only been a few notches down the 'pain-o-meter' to that which I expect Harry's mother went through giving birth to him.

Harry was one of nine children and in order of age they were; Thomas, Harry, Edith, Levi, Samuel, Myra, Josiah, Alice and George. Their dad was a Foundry Worker so I would imagine times would have been pretty tough for them. Similarly a 1911 census describes Harry and two of his brothers, Thomas and Levi, as being General Labourers at a Tube Works. Perhaps they worked in the same foundry as their dad.

His younger sister Edith, who was sixteen at the time, was a Nail Maker. My nan, who was born thirteen years after Harry and from a big family of seven children, has told me on many occasions that quite often when she was very young she would go without food. There simply wasn't enough to go around. She remembers some days making sure she passed the local bakery on the way to school just so she could stare at the fresh bread and cakes through the window. Also if you had a pair of shoes back then, you kept them until they were beyond repair or you were handed down some more from an older sibling. So, all together, a bit of a struggle, but the Hacketts were a big family. Perhaps this was a benefit as they could all help each other in times of need.

I'm afraid that's the entire extent of my knowledge about Harry as a youngster, however I do know a little more about Harry's army days.

All of the information I have pulled together is made up of a few anecdotes from family members; some facts based on research I've carried out; as well as the chronological material I've received from the Grenadier Guards in the form of his official Service Record. Every soldier has one of these and it details all the notable events during a person's life in the armed services. One can be requested by contacting the regiment of any soldier or sometimes by searching online. At first I'd struggled with how exactly to flesh out the Service Record data, as it's just a list of dates with a few hand-written notes next to them. Some of the sentences have abbreviated 'army code' and it can take a little detective work to figure out what some of them mean. I especially didn't want these date-led events to appear like a huge diary as that would be more boring than staring at the inside of your own eyelids for hours on end. To avoid this I decided to intersperse these dates with various WW1 facts and tales that I'd come across. Most of this was from reading books on the subject and during a few visits I'd made to the battlefields of Northern France. While writing this I also decided to season this fairly static information with a little light conversational detail and at times seemingly unrelated banter.

Every young lad dreams of being a soldier

I remember, quite vividly, playing 'army' when I was a kid. At school this was generally during 'play-time' when I would link arms with my best buddy and simply stomp through the playground singing, 'who wants to join our army gang?' over and over again. As you did this your ranks would swell as new recruits joined your mass 'Tiller-Girl-esque' line up. The chant would continue with the occasional deviation in the lyrics as follows; 'Who wants to join our army gang? NO GIRLS!' This was simply because, of course, school-yard army business was far too serious and 'roughtie-toughtie' for girls. Once we had reached critical mass, we would then split into two groups, generally 'Americans' and 'Germans'. After we had agreed when the war would start, we'd all run for cover until one side decided it was time to launch an all-out attack. The attack had to be seen to be believed. What seemed like 300 (but was, in fact, about twelve) 'Germans' would rush the 'Americans' and proceed to belt out their own home-grown best possible machine-gun, rifle and bomb sounds. They ranged from your standard 'tat-tat-tat-tat-tat-tat-tat', to your 'pee-oww-pee-oww-pee-oww', the lightning fast tongue rolling 'durr-r-r-r-r-r-r-r-r-r' or your more subdued 'duh-duh-duh-duh-duh-duh-duh'. Occasionally one of the more creative kids would lob in the odd 'invisible' hand grenade with an impressive, 'Weeeeeeeeeeeeeeee-dooooom-kablooshaaaaa!' It was mayhem and there would be bodies everywhere, until the end of play-time bell rang to signal the end of hostilities. We'd all then spring to our feet, dust ourselves off, decide who had won (usually the Americans) and file back into class.

I loved playing army. I think it was just because you could run around like a 'nutjob', making crazy gun and explosion noises while occasionally diving to the floor and rolling around in pretend agony as if you'd been shot to pieces by a 'pesky German'. There was one lad who was king of 'army' at our school. He had perfected the 'mother' of all one-man cannon sounds that could easily account for the annihilation of at least six or seven kids with one deep, booming 'THA-GA-BA-DOOOOM'. He was a 1970's version of 'Terminator' and way ahead of his time. For the lads, 'army' was usually the top game at our little school. That was, of course, until we got bored or a new 'fad' came to town, such as 'marlies' or 'klackers' or those bendy plastic tubes that you used to spin around your head to make a whooping, whistling sound. This last one didn't last long as the teachers where convinced you could easily have someone's eye out when spinning them at 200 miles an hour. So, naturally, they got banned from school before there was a mass 'blinding'.

In reality I can't actually recall, at any time in my life, having any inclination to join any of the actual armed forces. Except perhaps once.

I was in my first year of secondary school. It would have been when a soldier gave a presentation during a careers-focus day. He explained what it was like to be in the real army. After hearing him talk about fabulous weapons, tanks, suntans, adventures and far-off exotic places, I thought, 'I'm liking the sound of that'. Two seconds later I had a re-think and my brain had a short but serious conversation with itself. The results were in and my mind made up. I had spotted a serious down-side. The decision was made. It was; 'No, a career that involves being potentially properly shot at or blown to smithereens, is not for me'. Instead I decided on a far less violent profession. I wanted to be... a circus clown. But even to this day I can't for the life of me remember why. I think it's because it looked a doddle and involved faffing around wearing huge trousers and badly fitting enormous shoes. You were also allowed to beat your colleagues with huge fake frying pans, and best of all, you got paid to do it. Plus you had no chance of being shot at. I also remember lying through my teeth and telling the teachers, when asked if I'd thought of a career path, that I fancied becoming a school teacher just like them. But I don't think I ever told anyone about my painted-face, custard-pie throwing aspirations after that.

Fortunately this ambition petered out and I bumbled into computers shortly after leaving secondary school. Similarly, and not many people know this, my wife Jacqui was, at one point very seriously considering joining the military when we were going out as teenagers. She visited the recruiting office, had the 'soldier-to-teenager' chat, studied all the literature and was only a step or two away from actually going for it. Like I had, Jacqui decided against this profession. I'm glad she did as I would have been lost without her for months on end while she was off fighting people and working on her suntan. I remind her of this fact every now and then by calling her 'Private Benjamin'.

It seems that in stark contrast to me, Harry had well and truly chosen his career path because he enlisted on 5 July 1911 well before the outbreak of WW1. This would indicate that he had made a conscious decision to become a professional soldier. He wasn't enticed by the, yet to come, thrill of a convenient 'over-before-Christmas' war. Neither had he been conscripted and made to join up, as others were, once war broke out. He signed up for the minimum three-year term. This meant he would have been known as a Regular in 'army-speak' once he had signed on the dotted line. There would have been several options open to him with a choice of local regiments to join. Generally people used to join those closest to home. In Harry's case you would have expected him to link up with one of those that were all very close to the Black Country. However Harry chose to join The Grenadier Guards who were based miles away 'down south'.

Now, for me, the mention of the Grenadier Guards immediately 'pings' a picture in my mind of those super-smart, super-tall select few who stand, statuesque and motionless, outside Buckingham Palace. Their uniform is unmistakable; a red tunic, white belt, immaculate brass buttons and of course the essential 'king of all head gear', the bearskin. As a youngster one of my favourite toys was my Action Man. I had several outfits ranging from astronauts to frog-men but the suit I loved the most was the Grenadier Guard outfit. It just looked so smart and regal. This uniform is precisely what Harry would've been expected to wear when he performed Guards ceremonial duties in our nation's capital. Signing up to the Grenadiers' Regiment was pretty special and meant that you were part of what was accepted back then as the elite of the British Army. They were, after all, 'His Majesty's Guards', the prime regiment with the finest record on the battlefield and traditions and purpose that stretched way back.

He was assigned to the 1st Battalion and his enlistment document clearly states he was 'twenty years and six months old, with a fresh complexion, grey eyes, brown hair and standing five feet eleven and a half inches tall'. This last point may have been why he was referred to the Guards, the minimum height being at that time five feet ten inches. They looked out for and recruited all the tall chaps. Prior to joining the Guards he had also spent some time with the more local 7th Battalion Worcestershire Regiment in the Territorial Force, so he would have had a fair taste of army life. It sounded like this young man really did want to be a soldier.

New recruits at that time were based and trained at the Caterham Depot, which is about twenty miles south of London in Surrey. This depot was also affectionately referred to by Grenadiers as 'Little Sparta'. Sparta was an ancient Greek city-state famed for particularly rigorous military training and was the centre of their vast military powers. At 'Little Sparta' the new Guards would be taught 'drill' which is simply marching. Marching doesn't sound like much of a skill for a fighting man to have, however it was vitally important to soldiering. Why? Because all the most powerful, efficient, successful empires throughout history had to have fully developed methods for moving massive, organised units of troops from one place to another. They didn't have motorised armoured troop carriers or Chinook helicopters. It was essential that on the battlefield you kept your blokes together and avoided individuals getting lost or mixed up with other units. This makes perfect sense, I suppose. Along with drill training and physical fitness they'd be instructed in the various regimental traditions and proud history. Above all Harry would be taught how to obey orders, fight wars and literally knock the stuffing out of sacks full of straw with an 18-inch (46 cm) bayonet. And, of course, Grenadier Guards, like any foot soldiers throughout the ages, were trained, first and foremost, how to kill. It sounds harsh put like that but it is the truth. The top of any list of required attributes for a soldier had to be 'must be willing to protect King and Country and kill people'.

It's worth pointing out here that Guard's training was tough, unforgiving and in some cases very brutal. That might sound a little odd as it was peacetime after all. But wars are not nice tidy, gentlemanly affairs. Those in command of soldiers have to be sure of one thing. That when they issue an order, it will be obeyed to the letter. In the midst of battle, the fog of war, the fear and confusion, if soldiers are ordered to advance, they must advance. No questions. No, 'But Sir, do you really think that's wise, Sir, it looks an awfully tricky situation?' or 'Sir, but there are more of them than us, Sir!' They have to obey. This conditioning comes at a price and I have read actual accounts of Sergeant Majors in the Guards who have pushed and pushed the men under their charge to breaking point. Even during peace-time in training. Soldiering is a rough, tough profession; even today it's not a career anyone takes on lightly. New recruits came out of Little Sparta tough, fit, highly-disciplined, professional fighting men.

The present day Guards Regiment can be traced to its origins in 1656 in Bruges, Belgium where it formed part of the bodyguard for the exiled English King Charles II. A few years later in 1665 it merged with another regiment to form the 1st Regiment of Foot Guards and since then they have served under ten Sovereigns. The term Grenadier was first used in 1815 honouring the part they played in defeating the 'Grenadiers of the French Imperial Guard' at the Battle of Waterloo. The regiment's motto is the French, 'Honi soit qui mal y pense' or 'Evil be to him who evil thinks' and the Colonel of the Regiment today is HRH The Duke of Edinburgh. Nowadays the overall Guards Divisions consist of Grenadier, Coldstream, Scots, Irish and Welsh Guards.

Harry must've fitted in and done very well because on 20 June 1912, just over twelve months after joining up, he was promoted from Guardsman, which is 'Grenadier-speak' for Private, to Lance Corporal. The rank of Lance Corporal sits between Private and full Corporal, it's basically the bottom rung of the Non-Commissioned Officer ladder. Lance Corporals generally act as second-in-command of a section of around eight to thirteen men. A month after his promotion Harry opted to extend his service from three to seven years with 'the Colours'. This is possibly for one of a few reasons. Firstly, he was loving being in the Guards. Secondly, he'd probably get a little more respect from the more established officers. Thirdly, most significantly, seven years showed commitment to a long haul. Without this there was little chance of further promotions.

Just for background, a Non-Commissioned Officer (NCO) would usually obtain his position of authority by working his way up via promotion through the enlisted ranks. Whereas a Commissioned Officer, (CO) would be slotted directly into the officer corps. At the time of WW1 a CO would have probably come from what would have been seen as the upper-class or well-educated set.

Harry was trained in the particular skill of range-finding, which meant that he'd be required to carry a special instrument that would assist with ensuring rifles and guns were 'tuned' to their intended targets. On St Valentine's Day 1914 Harry was promoted yet again, another notch up the ladder, becoming a full Corporal. This rank allowed him to wear two chevrons as insignia on each sleeve of his uniform. Goodness knows what his company must have thought of him when he was barking out orders with his thick, Black Country accent. I dare say it raised a few comments such as, 'What the heck did he just say, is he a Brummie by any chance?'

If you've ever seen a typical photograph of a British Infantry soldier you will probably have noticed the khaki and heavy-gauged material uniform, the rifle, (maybe even with a bayonet), the unmistakable round 'tin hat', known as a Brodie helmet, and you might even have noticed the unusual bandage-like wrappings from his boots to his knees, known as puttees. What you probably wouldn't notice would be the rest of his gear considered standard issue. This would include; a knapsack (like a messenger-bag come rucksack), water bottle, webbing (this is the thick belt and shoulder harness used to attach some of the other gear to), Mills bombs (grenades), entrenching tool (spade to you and me), ammunition pouches, gas mask and rain cape. They reckoned all the gear amounted to around 27 kilograms or 60 lbs in 'old money'.

You'd be right if you thought that a fully 'tooled-up' soldier looked awkward and clumsy with all that paraphernalia hanging off him. But at the time, and I'd say around the end of 1917, this gear was absolutely state-of-the-art. There was nothing better on the market. Everything had a purpose and was fitted to the webbing to provide an efficient, easy to put on and remove 'fighting-wardrobe'. I know it doesn't look it but on careful examination and explanation it really was 'ahead of the game'.

The key 'device' of any front line soldier is of course his weapon. In World War One it's been said, rightly or wrongly, that; the Germans built a hunting rifle; the Americans built a target rifle; but the British built a battle rifle. Allow me to attempt to explain. The German standard issue field rifle was the Mauser Gewehr 98. It was very well made, a great piece of engineering and a fine weapon. The American's Springfield rifle, was also well made with particular attention paid to the sights for aiming. The British rifle was built to do all of the above in measure, but also to withstand the rigours and mal-treatment on the battlefield. In comparison it was slightly more reliable when dirty and was above all designed to load bullets quickly using the rapid-fire bolt action. Back then an infantryman's rifle was not automatic so each round had to be manually loaded by means of a mechanical bolt action. The real advantage of the British rifle was that a soldier could aim down the barrel, shoot and reload without having to break focus with his target or move the gun from where it would have been tucked into his shoulder. This meant that ten rounds, which would have been the entire contents of his magazine of bullets, could be fired in rapid succession without him having to re-locate the target, re-aim and then fire. This is one of the reasons the Grenadiers could rapid-fire fifteen rounds a minute and why the Germans sometimes thought they were facing machine-guns. This British rifle was called the Lee Enfield. It became simply referred to as the '303' and made by Birmingham Small Arms or BSA in Armoury Road, Birmingham at the rate of 10,000 a week.

No one could know that, less than six months after Harry was promoted to Corporal, miles away from Little Sparta, in a seemingly insignificant place called Sarajevo an, until then, equally insignificant foreign Archduke would be assassinated. It was 28 June 1914 and this little ripple was destined to become a raging tsunami. The repercussions down the line resulted in, of all things, Britain declaring war on Germany on Tuesday 4 August 1914. This chain of events would change things, forever.

The Letters

In WW1 it was a usual activity for those serving to keep in touch with friends, family and loved ones by sending letters. Harry and Olive were no exception and they exchanged numerous letters, postcards and parcels before and during the war. Several letters sent from Harry to Olive have been carefully preserved over the years and excerpts of some of them have been reproduced where appropriate in order to help tell 'Harry's Story'.

Considering their age the letters and postcards are in great condition. Some are written on official YMCA, Salvation Army or note paper of all shapes and sizes. The hand-writing is consistent, informal and very neat. Some are written in ink and others in pencil. Any of the earlier letters Harry wrote in pencil carry a PS to apologise for him not being able to find any ink! I've selected a handful of anecdotes and excerpts which don't really do justice to the depth of feelings and polite personal conversations. Several of these selections appear throughout this book. If anything within them is shown in brackets [like this], then it signifies some interpretation or guidance that I've added for clarification.

These letters are unique and having survived almost 100 years, they are an absolute treasure. They are a 'time capsule' allowing a glimpse into a private world of hopes, love, fear, frustration, duty, sadness and the incredible first-hand experiences of Harry's war. I would urge you, if I may, to take time to study and 'take them in'. Most of them were written whilst on active duty in, or close to, the terrifying trench warfare of the Western Front. The words and grammar are just how they appear written down and in order to maintain their impact and authenticity they remain unedited. Above all they are Harry's distinctive words and by reading them I hope they allow you to 'connect' with him in some tangible way.

During the summer of 1914 Harry was making plans to travel home and for Olive to meet him and his family in Old Hill. He'd sent several letters outlining the trains to catch, the cost and which stations to transfer at. His planning was pretty detailed and left nothing to chance, it was obvious Harry wanted to make sure 'his Olive' was safe so he meticulously planned the journey. It must have been important to him and he was obviously looking forward to spending time with her. On 27 July 1914, from the Tower of London where he was on guard duty, he wrote the following which starts with his standard greeting of;

"Dearest Olive. I thought I would just drop you a line…"

And continues;

"…I hope you will be able to catch the 11:05 train alright, but mind you do not get into the wrong part of the train, as there are generally slip carriages on the rear part which stop at Leamington…Book right through from Paddington to Old Hill as it will save you the trouble of going up those stairs at Snowhill [a railway station in Birmingham]. *You remember where the booking office is don't you?..Do not forget what I told you about crossing over*

the bridge at Old Hill Station. I expect she [Myra, Harry's aunt] *will be waiting for you...go down the steps and wait at the bottom of the station gates. I think she will be able to tell you from your photograph".*

For me, reading these few simple lines has a particular significance as I use the two stations mentioned twice a day during my commute to the office. It's nothing earth-shattering I know but it does amplify the link I feel with Harry and Olive.

Two days later, again from the Tower of London, he rather ominously wrote;

"I am sorry to say dear Olive that I do not think I shall be able to come [to Old Hill] *at all on account of the war which has broke out in Serbia, we are now under orders to be ready at any minute. There was some of our Company sent away last night to Scotland to guard some big oil tanks which are there and they say that we may be sent away on Friday. There is still time for them to settle things and you may guess that I shall come over if there is the least chance of doing so. I think myself that it will all fall through before it affects us...There are only about a hundred of us left here now out of the whole battalion..."*

Once war was declared, the British Armed forces across the globe were primed and made ready to 'do their duty for King and Country'. None of them had any idea what war would look or feel like in the industrialised world of the early 20th century.

In the middle of September, in order to respond to the requirements of the new war, a huge military unit was formed known as the 7th Division. This Division, along with several others, was part of the fighting force forever associated with Britain and the First World War. It was the British Expeditionary Force or B.E.F.

At the time it was accepted without doubt by the Government and the British Army that this new 7th Division was one of the finest fighting forces ever assembled. Many of its soldiers had served for several years in the far-flung colonies of the British Empire. They were fighting fit and bronzed, at the top of their game, highly experienced professional soldiers.

A Division, in military terms, is how the army organises itself into a coherent fighting force. It is made up something similar to this: a

Division has around 15,000 men, a Brigade 5,000, a Battalion 1,000 then down to just over 200 men in a smaller group known as a Company. The 1st Battalion Grenadier Guards, along with Harry, were part of the 20th Brigade who were, in turn, part of this new 7th Division. They were mobilised and moved to Lyndhurst near the New Forest in Hampshire ready for their orders to board a ship and cross the channel.

Light the blue touch-paper and retire a safe distance

I t's worth highlighting the events that started this war to end all wars in a little more detail. When you read the chain of events they seem far-fetched and almost unbelievable. It's worth noting that at around this time Britain and Germany were not the best of buddies. There was some kind of, 'mine's bigger than yours, power-struggle-funky-supremacy' tension between the two nations and this didn't help things at all. As mentioned before, it really was a domino effect, but the pieces seem unrelated and distorted. The pieces being: governments, rulers, egos and countries. Here are some key points to help explain the spark that led to four years of fireworks.

A country called Austria-Hungary declared war first in this series of events, on neighbouring Serbia. This was because the Austro-Hungarians had just taken over Bosnia. The people of Bosnia considered themselves Serbs and wanted Bosnia to be part of Serbia. Because of all this political uneasiness, a Serbian faction called the Black Hand Group decided to destabilise things and by-pass political diplomacy. They began by assassinating Austria's next in line to the throne while he was 'on tour' in Sarajevo. He was called Archduke Franz Ferdinand. Austria immediately blamed Serbia for this atrocity and sent them a weighty ultimatum listing several harsh political terms. They topped it off with a demand that all terms should be agreed by an unrealistic date and time. The Serbian government couldn't or wouldn't fulfil all the demands, so Austria simply declared war on Serbia.

The Austrian army then shelled Belgrade, the capital of Serbia. The Serbians mobilised, (called up their army), and asked their close ally

Russia for help. Russia decided to support them and subsequently ordered the mobilisation of their own troops.

Up until this point Germany had not been involved, but they were an ally of Austria-Hungary, so they decided to declare war on Russia for supporting Serbia. The alliance between Germany and Austria was a natural one, they both spoke the same language and had very similar cultures. In previous centuries, they had also both been part of the same empire, the Roman Empire. Germany also demanded that France 'keep its nose out of this fracas' and also it must 'declare itself neutral'. France being very French about it totally refused and mobilised their armed forces 'tout-de-suite'. Once they'd told Germany where to 'stick it', Germany replied by declaring war on them. Declaring war back then was a 'doddle'.

Finally on 4 August 1914 Germany invaded neutral Belgium as part of a wider plan to quickly take France out of the equation and bingo! Britain declared war on Germany in support of Belgium and France.

The tension I mentioned earlier between Britain and Germany was probably down to a couple of reasons. Around 1900, Britain had a governing involvement in a quarter of the world. The British Empire, as it was known, included countries such as Canada, India, South Africa, Egypt, Australia and New Zealand. Queen Victoria had also been crowned Empress of India. Huge amounts of money were made from these colonies and in order to protect her interests, Britain had a powerful military presence in all parts of the world. The Empire was seen as the status symbol of a country that was the most powerful in the world. Ever wondered why we are called 'Great Britain'?

Germany therefore clearly believed that a sign of great power was possession of overseas colonies. The best ones had already been taken by Britain but, politically, they resolved as a nation to gain as much colonial territory as possible. This led to them dabbling and colonising territory in Southern Africa.

Another issue that caused much hostility between Britain and Germany was, believe it or not, Germany's desire to increase the size of her navy. Britain accepted that Germany, as a large land-based country, needed a large army. But they had a very small coastline and Britain couldn't accept that Germany needed a large navy. Britain had a huge navy and at the time 'Britannia really did rule the waves'. Britain concluded that

Germany's desire to increase the size of her navy was in order to threaten Britain's naval might in the North Sea. The British governments position was that as an island we needed a large navy and they could not accept any perceived challenge in that department from Germany. As a result, a naval building race ensued. Both countries poured disgusting sums of money into building new warships and those costs soared when Britain launched a new state-of-the-art battleship called the Dreadnought. Germany immediately responded by building her own equivalent 'Das Even Bigger And Better Than Yours Dreadnought'. This reaction did little to improve relations between Britain and Germany. All it did was to fuel the already smouldering tensions between the two European powers.

With these two nations at odds with each other, it only needed one tiny incident to spark off a disaster. The incident, we identified earlier, was that 'ripple' back in Sarajevo.

Every soldier yearns for a bit of real action...don't they?

I wanted to check out the validity of the heading to this section so I thought I'd ask a good friend of mine what he thought. Dan Treby was until recently in 42 Commando Royal Marines. As part of his training he specialised in using a GPMG (General Purpose Machine Gun). In battle he'd be one of the lads responsible for spraying the enemy with 750 rounds-per-minute at ranges of up to 1800 metres. Back in WW1 our standard Lewis machine-gun, made by BSA, still fired a respectable 500 to 600 rounds-per-minute but typically required a six to eight-man team to operate. One to fire; one to feed the ammunition; the rest to help carry the weapon its ammunition and spare parts. I remember Dan telling me he used to carry his GPMG on his hip ready to fire when out on patrol. Proper 'Call of Duty' computer war-game stuff. So, to find an answer to my question I asked him one day point-blank. 'Dan, when you were in the Marines, did you really expect to be shipped out at a moment's notice and have to defend yourself and maybe lay into whoever the enemy might be with your GPMG?' He didn't hesitate and said, 'Absolutely yes. Everyone in the team knew exactly what they'd been trained to do and wouldn't hesitate to do what was expected of them. It was our job and our duty'.

On 31 July 1914 Harry, who was still based in London, was unsure of where he would be posted. He wrote again from guard duty at the Tower of London;

"...we have been awaiting orders to move since yesterday morning, all the company moved off to Newcastle except nine of us yesterday. The reason I did not go is because I was on guard and there was no one to relieve us until more troops came in from Wellington Barracks...this place is all upside down, nobody knew anything about moving until 9 o'clock yesterday morning and at half past ten they were on their way to Newcastle leaving all the kits thrown all over the show. We have now got everything packed away, ready to move at any moment".

This uncertainty about whether he would be sent off to war continued and on 3 August he wrote;

"My Dearest Olive. I received your letter alright this morning as we are still at the Tower, although they keep sending parties of men away to different places. But I do not now expect they will send me anywhere unless the whole battalion goes, as I do not have a rifle only for drill duties. I am what we call the Company Range Taker that is a special instrument which is used to tell how far off any object is and we have to carry this instrument about with us. They give us revolvers instead of rifles...I expect you will know by the papers tonight what part England is taking in this crisis. But no matter where I go I shall always be thinking of you and I know you will of me...With truest and best love, Harry".

Harry mentions his role as Company Range Taker. There were generally five per Battalion: one for each company and one for the machine gun section. The kit he had to carry was a cumbersome rangefinder complete with tripod. It was used to monitor targets through a dual eyepiece so that officers or NCO's could give ranges for sighting their weapons.

His correspondence continues to explain his situation. He had been moved from London to Warley Barracks, Brentwood, Essex. Whilst there in a letter dated 8 August 1914 he begins to introduce a sense of concern regarding the future;

"Dear Olive I suppose you know by now that we have mobilised. We were fetched from the docks last night to get ready for active service and I suppose we shall be off tomorrow or Sunday. They have called up all the reserves and the barracks were over crowded...there are rumours we are only for coastal defence and others say we are going with that Expeditionary Force to Belgium...I must once again give my promise that is, I will be yours and only yours whatever happens and should we not meet again, you will know that I have been true to the end. I have no doubt whatever that this country will be victorious. I am sure that the Germans have asked for it".

While at Warley he also made the following remarks about a very important 'new recruit';

"...I shall not be sorry when I leave this place, we are all packed together like a tin of sardines...The Prince of Wales joined us this morning [16 August 1914] *and has been out training with us. Of course we only pay compliments to him the same as we do any other officer. He is a nice young chicko* [a term meaning lad] *and seems like a school boy amongst all the other officers".*

"...there is a rumour we go to Wellington Barracks tomorrow (Thur)...they say we are being inspected by the King and then go over to France with the first draft probably sometime next week...I hardly seem to realise what this is going to mean to us...still, I know you will be thinking of me and that is helping me to keep a good heart".

As Harry had hinted towards the end of August they were all moved back to Wellington barracks, just across from Buckingham Palace, in London where four battalions were readied for inspection.

On 23 August he informs Olive that for some reason he had volunteered for a new preventative treatment;

"...I have hardly been able to walk about since Friday afternoon as I have been inoculated. They came round during this week wanting to know who would volunteer to be done and of course I gave my name in. This inoculation is something similar to vaccination only I think a thousand times more painful. They inject some stuff into your blood...I have been through the mill for this last two days".

Eventually, early in September 1914, Harry and the Grenadiers were moved to a huge temporary tent-style camp at Lyndhurst near to Southampton. Here, they were kept 'at the ready' waiting to be shipped out at a moment's notice to do their duty and fight a war. Harry continued his letter writing to his sweetheart at every opportunity. It must have been a little frustrating knowing that you were so very close to crossing the Channel but you also had no idea of when that might actually be. I dare say most soldiers just wanted to get over there and get stuck in. Here are a few of Harry's thoughts and experiences during this time;

"Well Dearest Olive I am pleased to say I am alright and hope you are. We are waiting for a battalion of Scots to come from Egypt before we move off and they are expected the end of next week...I must say I am getting on as well as can be expected under the circumstances. There are about twenty thousand troops down here altogether and some Territorials which are doing training...there are about twelve thousand who go out with us, there are three battalions belonging to our brigade the 20th. 1st Battalion Grenadier Guards, 2nd Battalion Scots Guards and a battalion of the Border regiment and we are now waiting for a battalion of the Gordon Highlanders to come from Egypt...the name of our commander is General Capper a very nice fellow".

Like anyone in an uncertain situation Harry begins to think of the future;

"Dear Olive we have got to look forward now to the time when we can get settled down again and perhaps I may be able to leave the army a short time after the war is over, then we may be able to settle down to things a bit better...with truest and fondest love, from yours only, Harry".

The time in Lyndhurst was put to good use by the officers and the troops were exercised and constantly put through their paces as Harry explains;

"...I have not wrote to anyone since Sunday except you as I have not had time, we got up at 4:30am this morning and went out at 5:30am and did not return until nearly 4 o'clock this afternoon so you see how things have been..."

On 21 September, still at the 'tented-camp' he wrote;

"It is now said Dear Olive we go to the front next Sunday leaving here about 7 o'clock at night. I have had some cigarettes sent me by Uncle Levi and also a letter from home, they wish me to remember all of them to you...well Dearest I cannot write more tonight as I want to go into the village to get a pair of boots mended..."

Finally apologising for *"writing this in black lead as I am writing in the tent"* he announces;

"Well Dearest we have had at last some official news about going and so I move off [from Lyndhurst camp] *tomorrow and we go* [sail] *between Sunday and Tuesday"*.

So, after a period of hanging around waiting for orders it was decided to send the 7th Division to support the Belgian Army which was getting a severe pummelling in Antwerp by the Germans. On 4 October 1914 Harry and his Battalion marched from Lyndhurst to the docks at Southampton. In what appears to be a hastily written note dated 4 October 1914 he pens;

"My Dearest Olive I am writing these few lines just to let you know that at last we are going out. I am at present on board a troop ship at Southampton coming here early this morning. We set sail at 2 o'clock this afternoon but do not know where we are bound for".

"We marched from Lyndhurst to here and all along the roads were crowded. We had a very good reception and one I shall never forget. I should think I shook hands with over a thousand different people. Well dearest I will write when I get over the other side if I get a chance. This will be my last one in England for a time, still I am as happy as ever hope you are also. Must close as duty calls, I expect I shall be over there by the time you get this letter cannot get stamps. With my deepest and truest love, from your loving boy Harry xxx".

They then set sail for the port of Zeebrugge on the Belgian coast. They sailed aboard the cargo liner S.S. Armenian that had actually been converted for use to war-time horse transport. This vessel was under the management of the White Star line, who you might recall owned The Titanic. The journey would have been uncomfortable and perilous as they would have had to 'tip-toe' across the Channel in order to avoid enemy mines and the deadly U boats (German submarines) reported to be on the prowl. Sadly, less than a year later while performing other duties, the S.S. Armenian was torpedoed and sunk off the North Cornwall coast by U boat U-24. The crew abandoned ship and twenty-nine American crew members lost their lives. In addition 1,400 mules that were being shipped from the United States, for service somewhere on the Western Front, were also drowned. Anything, be it man, machine or beast supporting the war effort, was fair game to German U boats. The wreck remains upright on the sea bed about ninety-five metres below the surface. It is a known to scuba divers as 'The Bone Wreck' due to the fact that it is a macabre, under water, mule graveyard.

Harry's 20th Brigade was formed mainly from Grenadiers who until recently had been serving overseas. Only some of these units had returned to England following the outbreak of war and as a result of waiting for the others to return the 7th division was the last to arrive in Flanders, just in time for a momentous clash known as the First Battle of Ypres.

Just popping off to war, I'll be back by Christmas

After two days at sea Harry disembarked and the battalion assembled in Belgium ready to join the rest of the B.E.F. As mentioned earlier, the 7th Division had been given orders to assist in the defence of Antwerp, but the city had fallen before the Division even had the chance to get there and get 'stuck in'. Instead they were tasked with holding key important bridges and other routes that would assist the evacuation of the poor displaced Belgian civilians and their army, who were marching west. As soon as the Belgians were safely through, the Division were themselves ordered to move westwards. The Division dug in just near the Belgian city of Ypres. They would have been the first British troops to set foot in and occupy what was to become an infamous region forever associated with WW1.

It was here that Harry became directly engaged in battle, or more accurately series of battles, in and around West Flanders (Flanders is an area that covers the South of Belgium and the North of France).

It is at this point that Harry's letters reflect the shock and reality of warfare as he is well and truly 'in the thick of it';

"28 October 1914. My Dearest Olive. As we have a day rest after about ten days hard fighting I will try and write you a few lines...I think I have been rather lucky, I can hardly explain to you Olive what it has been like. I never thought anything could happen the same as I have seen this last few days. There was about eighty casualties in my company in one day and we have lost five of six officers. I hardly know how I got through it all myself...about four times as many Germans as there were us, still their losses were far more serious than ours. In fact we were told that their dead were piled up so high in front of their trenches that they could not see to fire over them. I cannot tell you all that has happened in this letter Olive but I shall never forget the sight and I do not think it is possible to go through much worse than we have done".

In the same letter with a note of optimism Harry says";

"...Olive I do not think it will last more than another six months and perhaps less than that".

These early battles would become known as the First Battle of Ypres. The British commanders were totally unaware of the sheer size of the German force advancing on the small medieval town. However, numbers alone would not overcome the highly trained, experienced, professional British soldiers. It was standard procedure to train regulars to be able to fire fifteen rounds (bullets) in sixty seconds from their standard issue Lee Enfield rifles. As mentioned before when this was deployed effectively in numbers the enemy often thought they were facing machine-guns due to the continuous tut-tut-tut-tut rhythm and torrent of bullets. This kind of concentrated fire-power was deadly when used against troops advancing in lines. Of course, Harry and the professionals would have spent hours upon hours on the target range practising what they called the 'mad minute' at Little Sparta. Then targets were made of wood and sacks of sand. Now their bullets would be finding flesh and splitting bone. I doubt anything fully prepared them for firing at real people for the first time.

In one battle account, the German advance in this area was made up of huge numbers, albeit young inexperienced recruits. Their task was to attack the far more battle-savvy professional British soldiers based north of the town at a place called Langemark. As they advanced towards the British, for the first time, they 'tasted' the firepower and resolve of the British Army in combat. 1,500 Germans were killed and 600 taken prisoner. The result was a victory for the B.E.F. Although it should be noted of course that losses were extremely heavy on both sides. The Germans called this battle 'The Massacre of the Innocents of Ypres' as most of their casualties were students and a mixture of young un-tested reserves. Some were reported to have only been between sixteen and seventeen years old. They approached the British lines in threes arm-in-arm with only one rifle between them.

Fierce fighting continued to take place all around Ypres and neither the British nor the Germans could claim to control the area. Nearby, about ten miles south of a town called Wijtschate (in Tommy-speak Whitesheet), a German corporal, whom you may have heard of, called Adolf Hitler rescued a wounded comrade. In doing so he won the Iron Cross, the highest honour a German soldier could be awarded.

Despite fearsome losses on both sides, neither side could gain the upper hand. Brutal battles continued to interrupt the once quiet rural landscape as they each struggled for supremacy. These early battles would have been a wake-up call, a brutal baptism of fire for everyone involved. War on this scale was new. Explosions as big as churches, swarms of unstoppable bullets, the ideally suited stumpy tubes of trench mortars that could drop bombs vertically into the midst of fighting men.

The 1st Battalion Grenadier Guards notably fought a successful delaying action on the Broodseinde Ridge during October. This battle in particular inflicted massive numbers of casualties on the German Army. The 7th Division stayed at Ypres for quite some time, fighting near Gheluvelt, Kruiseik Hill and Zillebeke. Between 14 October and 30 November 1914 the B.E.F. had sustained over 55,395 casualties. 7,960 were dead, 29,562 injured and a further 17,873 missing. Some British battalions simply didn't exist anymore as they were down to a handful of men. In particular Harry's 1,000-strong Battalion was reduced to just 4 officers and 200 men! Just take a moment to consider that. Over 75%, or three in every four, of your fellow men lost in a matter of weeks. It's hard to fathom. Our highly trained professional army were quickly being erased by overwhelming German numbers and violence. You can see why this war is viewed with such incomprehension due to the vast loss of life, and we hadn't even got to the end of 1914 yet!

The 7th continued to fight an ever-advancing German army ferociously until it managed to put a stop to the invasion just short of Ypres. Every unit suffered hideous losses, and it was not until early in 1917 that it was considered in a fit and complete enough state to be considered back to full fighting strength. After the courageous, selfless part they played in the First Battle of Ypres, the Division is always referred to as the 'Immortal Seventh'. About twenty kilometres west of Ypres there is a Memorial to the Division comprising a tall obelisk bearing the legend '7' on all four sides. The plaque on it reads, 'To the memory of our comrades of the 7th Division who fell in the Great War 1914 to 1918'. The memorial, sited in Broodseinde, is very near to where some of the first trenches were dug by the British 7th Division in mid-October 1914. This area became known as the Ypres Salient.

So what of this 'Salient' point?

Any books about the Western Front will more than likely use the word 'salient'. It's an odd word and until recently I'd only ever heard it used in a phrase like '... and the salient point is...' where it referred to a point which needs highlighting. In military terms it refers to an area of the frontline that protrudes or sticks out from the more usual straight battle lines where the enemy is obviously facing you front on. In a salient you actually have the enemy on three sides. This is not good. Regrettably this is precisely what it was like around Ypres. The Germans could randomly squeeze off a few rounds on a machine-gun or lob shells (missiles) 'willy-nilly' into the salient knowing they were bound to hit someone or something causing damage, chaos and death.

What's more they could also actually fire at you from behind! Especially if you were at the front tip of the Salient. Basically, if you are fighting a war, a Salient is a bad place to be. You can now see that this is where the British Army would have been exposed to amplified German assaults and why so many were killed and never ever seen again. They were obliterated or buried alive. It was destruction on a mega-scale.

It's probably worth pointing out that 'British Expeditionary Force' is generally only used, in WW1 terms, to specifically refer to the forces present in France and Belgium prior to 22 November 1914 which marked the end of the First Battle of Ypres. It's also a sobering thought to consider the fact that by the end of 1914, after real vicious battles at Mons, Le Cateau, Aisne and Ypres the B.E.F. (and this would have been our entire real professional army), had been virtually wiped out. This was because the German Commanders were executing a well thought out plan to neutralise France. This would have probably ended the war very quickly indeed. This in-turn, would have changed the future shape of Europe entirely. That said, the B.E.F. succeeded in stopping the German plans dead in their tracks at a critical point in this new war.

It was also around this time that the German Emperor Kaiser Wilhelm, was reported to have been extremely 'miffed' that his glorious plan of attack and advance had been halted. He famously dismissed the B.E.F. as being a '...contemptible little army'. This title was embraced in later years by the survivors who were proud to call themselves 'The Old Contemptibles'. It's now used exclusively to honour these soldiers who 'were there at the kick off'. Their dogged and determined bravery stopped Germany in what was referred to as 'the race to the sea'. The objective of this 'race' was for them to hurriedly advance to try to gain control of the channel ports so that no supplies or manpower could be landed to support the British war effort. Once the ports were secure they would then advance, surround and capture Paris. This would have guaranteed a French surrender and it would have been 'game over'.

The end of these particular early battles in late 1914 marked the end of mobile operations where fighting would move from place to place quite quickly. Advances, defences and counter attacks had been the order of the day. This was about to change as both sides now started to, quite literally, dig in and the new more static Trench Warfare, that is synonymous with the First World War, took over.

Sniper 1 – Cloth Cap 0

Books about World War One refer, time and again, to the huge loss of life. It's worth trying to shed a little light on what this daily devastation meant for our troops on the Western Front.

All soldiers aren't deployed in the front-line trench, where all the action is, at the same time. There is a system of reserve troops in a support trench to their rear and then further support troops located some way behind them in the reserve trench. Past the reserve trenches would be the massive guns of the Artillery. These would have all been linked by Communications trenches, used so the troops could navigate the different layers of trench systems under cover. If you were in the support or reserve areas you were less likely to get shelled, but they were still very dangerous places to be. The real action is up at the Front-line 'sharp end' where you'd be exposed to constant shelling, daylight attacks, night raids along with the absolute joy of being sniped at as you made your way along the jagged, irregular trench systems. Sniping was almost a trench sport with sharp shooters racking up scores of kills. Just a couple of seconds in the wrong place at the wrong time and you would be spotted and shot at. Usually in the head of course. And, of course in those early days of the B.E.F. soldiers didn't have metal helmets as they weren't introduced until mid-1915. They just had had cloth caps to protect their heads. A cloth cap versus a bullet travelling at 740 metres per second? There can only be one winner. Just imagine how much protection this headgear would have offered if a shell landed nearby spewing out shards of shrapnel!

A shell's sole purpose is to knock 'the living daylight' out of you and everything around you. Its mission was to deliver damage, pain and death. Once it exploded on impact it would spew out fragments of shell and shards that would literally cut you into several large pieces. Along with this, its eardrum-shattering shock-wave wanted to shake you so violently that it would rupture your internal organs (while they were still inside you). It would toss you around like a dog would with a cuddly toy. That wasn't all. It wanted to rip you limb from limb or, if it was a 'biggie', ultimately vaporise you. There are hundreds of thousands of bodies that have never been found on the battlefields of

France and Belgium. This was due to bombs, mud or both. Each would conspire to drown or bury men alive never to be rescued or removed. A convenient, instant, undetectable grave.

These days I don't suppose there are any of us who have the slightest possible chance of fully comprehending what a full-blown shell-attack would have been like. There is just no way to replicate the sheer volume, adrenalin flood, deafness, disorientation, smell, confusion, helplessness and shock. I once saw an excellent drama, set in a WW1 dugout, at a local theatre. At the end the lights went out and they tried to simulate the thunderous booms and screeches of a shell attack. We were safe in our comfy red-velour seats but it did succeed in unnerving you and certainly made me jump a few times. Of course it was not really scratching the surface of the 'real deal' but it did give a slight smidgeon of a glimpse.

In the Great War, during particularly concentrated bombardments, it has been calculated that five shells could fall in every single square metre of the battlefield under attack. Shelling could last anything from a few minutes, to a few hours, to a few weeks. Just to give some idea of scale. The British had a selection of shells; take the 'eighteen pounder' for example; we fired 86 million of them during WW1.

If you 'copped' a 'normal' explosive-type shell direct you wouldn't really know a thing about it. You'd simply be a 'goner'. But in WW1 some shells contained a gruesome selection of the dreaded poisonous gases. Gas shells were a different kettle of fish. They made an eerie dull thud when they landed, followed by a gentle, lulling hiss. WW1 soldiers had front row seats when these diabolical deliveries belched out their murderous 'curtain' of chemicals. The effects were devastating and consisted of a mixture of blindness, burning, choking and guaranteed a slow, painful death. Gas was also particularly good at melting lungs (very slowly of course) from the inside out.

The first recorded gas attack was by the French army very early in August 1914. They used gas grenades containing, the un-spell-checkable, xylyl bromide against the Germans. The gas wasn't capable of killing anyone as it was only an irritant tear-gas. The French used it a little as a last resort to try to stop the unrelenting German advance. It was seen as nothing more than a desperate act rather than a pre-planned intent to use it as an air-borne killer. Similarly in October

1914, the Germans attacked Neuve Chapelle. It was here that they fired gas shells at the French containing a chemical that caused violent sneezing fits. Once again, the gas was not designed to kill but to incapacitate an enemy so that they were incapable of defending their positions. I'm sure there aren't too many of you reading this who don't know that WW1 gassing didn't stop at just sneezing fits.

It didn't take long before the Germans really went to town with this new combat option. They identified that poison gas was a superb medium for inflicting major discomfort and loss of life. At the Second Battle of Ypres on 22 April 1915 they took the use of gas to a whole new level when they used chlorine for the first time. French lookouts in the front line trenches in Ypres spotted a yellow-green cloud slowly, ambling towards them. The gas had been purposely dispensed from specially manufactured pressurised cylinders and plumbing systems dug into the German front line trenches. You couldn't blame the French for thinking at first it was the more commonly deployed smokescreen tactic meant to mask the movement of German troops. Because of this, all their troops in the area packed the front-line trenches ready for a fight, right in the path of the apparent 'smokescreen'. The impact of the chlorine gas was instant and devastating. The silent killer had simply wafted into the trenches, coiled around the faces of its unsuspecting prey and delivered an ungentlemanly, indefensible deathblow. The French soldiers who were still capable of running, along with their supporting Algerian comrades, bolted from the cloud in absolute terror.

The undisputed success of this attack from the new 'kid on the block' was clear for all to see. The silent killer had arrived and well and truly proved its worth as the mass-murdering, malevolent, weapon of choice.

It didn't take long for those working behind the scenes in military laboratories to come up with even better gas technologies. Their research and development delivered the 'delightful' Phosgene and the oddly-named Mustard gas. Each one had their own particular 'party-piece'. Phosgene was a little sneaky. After inhalation by its victim it didn't at first appear to have caused much damage. This is because it hadn't yet completed its work. Its initial job was to embed itself well within the respiratory system. It then 'beavered' away quietly for forty-eight hours deteriorating lungs resulting in imminent deliberate death.

There was no cure. Once breathed in, it was simply a matter of time. On the other hand Mustard gas was big in the 'blisters and blindness' department. Within hours of being exposed to it this stealthy parasite would cause internal and external blistering. The damage caused to the lungs and other internal organs was excruciating and, more often than not, fatal. Those who did happen to survive the ordeal were generally and cruelly blinded by this odourless gas.

It's a paradox that adversity, suffering and hardship often spawn brilliant creativity, hope and compassion. WW1 'did this in spades' and inspired some simply outstanding poetry. There are too many moving, descriptive examples to mention here. Nonetheless, one written by a famous British soldier called Wilfred Owen is worth just highlighting. Wilfred served in the trenches and witnessed first-hand the effects of gas on his pals. His poem 'Dulce et Decorum est' sums up its impact better than anything I have ever seen or heard. If you really want to catch a glimpse of the cruel characteristics of gas, it is well worth reading this poem in full. If you ever contemplate and study these things and try to imagine what it was like to stand in the shoes of those who were in the thick of it, you might possibly get some idea of what they experienced and endured. It's one of the things that comes to mind whenever I look at a photograph of Harry. I think to myself 'what on God's earth did you see, feel, hear, smell and touch, Harry?'

All about Ypres

There is an inspiring, well-known memorial in Ypres called The Menin Gate. I, like millions of others, have visited this impressive coliseum-like mausoleum to the missing. There's a road that passes through it and it's the main eastern exit point from Ypres town. In Great War times, every soldier in the area would have marched through where it now stands in order to fight in the Ypres Salient. More than this, The Menin Gate Memorial contains the individually hand-engraved names of 55,000 British soldiers who fought and died in the Salient but were never found. It was unveiled in 1927 and since then at 8:00pm sharp, (except for a blip during WW2), they close the road so that the Last Post memorial ceremony can take place. This happens every single evening, rain or shine, without fail.

Dignitaries, friends, families and visiting school children from around the world, lay wreaths on the inside steps of the Menin Gate to this day. Quite by chance the last time Jacqui and I were there, reading some of the handwritten notes attached to wreaths and flowers, she happened to notice a beautiful ring of poppies that had been left there by visitors from The Wordsley School which is near Stourbridge, West Midlands. We noticed this in particular because it's the very same school she had attended as a child. The Last Post ceremony is very moving and guaranteed to remind even the most hard-hearted of us the meaning of courage and the dreadful 'personality' of war.

Ypres is an aesthetically pleasing, strikingly beautiful medieval city. I'd describe the architecture as 'quaintly-gothic', dominated by a huge cathedral tower and a nearby belfry that can be spotted from miles around. I love cities with a focal point, a piazza or town square and Ypres has a 'corker'. It's based around the belfry of what is called the Cloth Hall or Grote Markt in local lingo. This huge structure was first built in the 13th century in order to facilitate the cloth industry and international trade. I say 'first built' as it was more or less flattened during WW1. And when I say flattened I mean almost completely demolished. Just the lower parts of the main belfry remained. More than that, the entirety of Ypres was also pulverised into literally piles of rubble, debris, shattered timber interspersed with shell holes gouged out of the earth. The only way to really appreciate what happened to it is by looking at photographs taken during and just after the war. Any photographs of the town would be sure to include the jagged, 'pointy-wreck' of the Grote Markt. There are myriads of images of it in various stages of destruction, generally with British Soldiers marching past. You can always tell the ones marching from the Salient as they are weary, dishevelled, lost-souls, hunched up like zombies.

During the war, hundreds of thousands of British and British Empire troops marched across the square past the ruins of the Grote Markt, down the Meensestraat, out through where the Menin Gate now stands and on towards the front line. For many, the next time they returned would be as a name on the walls of the memorial.

The city was so badly trashed that you'd have been forgiven for just leaving it as it was and moving a few miles to the north or south to start again. Fortunately for everyone the Belgian people didn't give up so easily. They completely rebuilt the Grote Markt and the rest of the buildings in the town brick by brick, carefully following salvaged original plans. Today the city is pristine and has a feel like no other place I've ever visited. The buildings seem ancient and authentic but are not. They have all been meticulously reconstructed. It is well worth a visit with many welcoming bars, hotels and shops. It's quite a tourist destination but, unlike anywhere else, people don't seem to be there for themselves ... if you know what I mean. They are there to remember and think of others, this is what gives it such a unique, gentle, calming atmosphere. If you ever get chance to visit, I'd highly recommend it. You can visit the 'In Flanders Fields Museum' based in the Grote Markt. It's a very stylish, contemporary facility that uses all kinds of new and old media to give visitors an appreciation and greater understanding of what took place in the area during WW1.

The people of the city seem very proud of their history and while they don't dwell or live in the past they do pay tribute and acknowledge the 'journey' of their home-town. One small example of this is a hotel Jacqui and I once stayed in called The Main Street Hotel. It is a fantastic place to stay and has a classy, unique style. In the reception they have a very impressive, distinctive clock that has been made from shell and bullet fragments found only recently in their own garden.

Harry and British soldiers fighting in The Salient would have witnessed the drawn-out, painful demolition of Ypres and more of the same in the front-line trenches, on a daily basis. The ones who survived the continuous onslaught would have most likely had to pick up the pieces of their shattered pals. It must have been like working in a nightmarish abattoir.

Welcome to my humble abode

If you were a front-line soldier in WW1 you would have eaten, slept, toileted, repaired your kit, fetched and carried, read letters, written replies and fought in a trench. Every one of these subterranean gulleys had to be dug by hand, to specific specifications. I used to think they were just dug in long lines but they weren't, for a very good reason. They were built with jagged bays every now and again so that if an enemy happened to 'pop in' with his rifle, he couldn't shoot straight down the length of the entire trench. Also, if a shell or grenade landed in the trench it would generally only affect the men in that section. If you looked at a trench from the air it would look kind of zigzagged. They had a bit at the front facing the enemy, called a parapet, and a bit at the back called a parados. The parados would be slightly higher than the parapet so that it would at least offer a little camouflage cover from the enemy if you did happen to pop your head above the parapet. If the trench was built to spec you would also be able to walk along it, on duckboards to keep your feet dry, again without being seen. But as they were the subject of inevitable shelling they'd more often than not be in a right state. So you might need to take care when moving about carrying out chores or visiting the delightful toilets (large bucket in a bay of the trench wall). They'd be repaired at night under the cover of darkness until a German 'Very' light or flare was sent up just to try and catch you out so they could spray you with their machine-guns.

Trenches also had their own special creature comforts. They would have been full of smelly men, rainwater, mud, fat rats gorged on human flesh, sludge, lice, stinks and bits of dead bodies. They would have been freezing in winter and boiling hot in summer time. To our troops they were their homes and, quite often, their graves.

During this early stage of the war (that they were convinced would be 'over before Christmas') most, if not all, must have started to have serious doubts that they'd ever be back home stuffing themselves with turkey and Christmas pud. They'd have witnessed the carnage and resistance first hand and any thoughts of a 'quick scrap then home to bask in the Glory back in England' were fading fast. The escalation of hostilities and casualties were showing no signs of letting-up. They were just getting started.

Less than three weeks after landing at Zeebrugge, Harry was promoted from Corporal to Sergeant. There's a chance that as soldiers were dropping like flies (remember earlier battles had wiped out 75% of Harry's 1,000 strong battalion) any promotions had to be carried out swiftly and ad-hoc in order to ensure the troops were properly 'managed'. Late in October 1914 the 1st Battalion moved from billets, which is what the military call temporary lodgings, outside Ypres to improvised shelters at a place a few miles away known as Sanctuary Wood. It's thought to have been given this name because early in the war, some soldiers had found shelter there. Or, in other words, been offered some-kind of sanctuary from a battle as they tried to make sense of where they were so they could return to their units. Following shelling in November, the name could hardly be considered appropriate. The only trees were stumps or shards and splinters bearing little or no resemblance to anything you could call a wood. But, the name stuck.

You can visit this area today and actually walk through some of the original preserved trenches. It's pretty over-grown now with mature trees but it still gives an idea of the trench layout and set up. There's also a small museum there with original artefacts, huge amounts of shell cases, bullet riddled trees and bent, rusty, disfigured metal. It's very quiet there apart from the occasional influx of European school kids on coach tours. In my opinion, when I visited, I felt it was a little 'spooky'.

The Western Front...was it ever quiet?

As the troops were rotated in and out of the front line or moved from section to section, this meant it wasn't always fighting, bombs, gas, murder, death, kill. There was always something going on and, as part of army protocols and rules, war diaries had to be kept and completed religiously to record activity. It was the responsibility of the commander of every military unit, from a battalion to a division, to ensure that the War Diary was kept up to date every day. It had to be written up each evening by a specific junior officer and usually signed off by a senior or commanding officer. Just to give you a view into a month with Harry in the 1st Battalion Grenadier Guards here are a few excerpts for December 1914 from the official war diary. I've replaced any 'army-speak' abbreviations with the actual words to make it easier to follow:

1 December 1914 - Commanding Officer visited the trenches in the morning.

3 December 1914 - Captain E O Stewart arrived with a draft of 66 men.

4 December 1914 - Major C Corkran proceeded to England on 10 days leave.

5 December 1914 - Brigadier went round our trenches.

6 December 1914 - Battalion was relieved by the Scots Guards and marched into billets near Sailly as Division reserve. Lieutenant Mitchell returned to duty from leave.

7 December 1914 - Battalion spent morning working and cleaning.

8 December 1914 - Battalion went for a route march through Sailly and back to billets by the Rue Quesnoy.

9 December 1914 - 2nd Lieutenant Darby returned to duty from leave.

10 December 1914 - Went back to the trenches to relieve the Scots Guards.

11 December 1914 - Rained hard during the night; trenches were in a bad condition.

12 December 1914 - Captain Douglas-Pennant and 45 other ranks joined the Battalion.

13 December 1914 - The Battalions line was extended to a full Companys distance of the right of No 2 subsection.

14 December 1914 - The Battalion was ordered to keep up a heavy rifle fire all day with the idea of keeping the enemy in their trenches. The Scots Guards relieved us in the evening and the Battalion marched back into Division reserve.

15 December 1914 - Battalion had use of the Divisions baths all day.

16 December 1914 - King's and 2nd Company were ordered to proceed to billets at the North East end of the Rue De Quesnes to dig at night on our new line of trenches.

17 December 1914 - 2nd Lieutenants Duberly, Rowley and Parker Jervis joined the Battalion also Lieutenant Greville with 60 men.

18 December 1914 - Received orders to go back in the trenches. The Scots Guards, Borders and 22nd Brigade made an attack in the evening. The Scots Guards took part of a trench about 25 yards in length but were forced to abandon it before morning; their casualties were 6 officers and 188 men. The total casualties in the Division amounted to 48 officers and 750 men. The Battalion held the trenches on the Right of the Scots Guards.

20 December 1914 - Lieutenant and Quartermaster Teece was wounded.

21 December 1914 - 2nd Lieutenants Sitwell, Burnand and Guthrie joined the Battalion.

23 December 1914 - Scots Guards relieved us in the trenches. 2nd Lieutenant Westmacott and 41 other ranks joined the Battalion.

24 December 1914 - Prince of Wales and General Officer Commanding 7th Division visited the Battalion.

25 December 1914 - Draft of 20 Non Commissioned Officers and men arrived.

26 December 1914 - Major Corkran went to hospital. Stood to arms about midnight owing to supposed night attack by the Germans.

27 December 1914 - Went back into the trenches to take up a new line with our left on the River Des Layes with our right on a point at present held by the left of the 8th Division.

28 December 1914 - No firing on either side, the Battalion spent the day in strengthening the line and at night a lot of work was done on the wire entanglements in front of the trench.

31 December 1914 - The Battalion was relieved in the trenches by the Scots Guards and went back into Divisional reserve. During the time the Battalion was in the trenches in the last 4 days a great many improvements were made in our line owing to the enemy not firing.

You'll notice that this period covers Christmas Day 1914, the date they thought the 'war to end all wars' would have been done and dusted by. It's also interesting to note the visit on Christmas Eve by the Prince of Wales who was an officer in the Grenadier Guards. This is the young Edward who became King Edward VIII and then, famously, abdicated in 1936. If you look carefully you can also count no fewer than 242 new men joining the battalion during this one month alone. These would be to replace some of those lost. More importantly it is just worth noting the few unusual reports of 'the enemy not firing' for a period just after Christmas Day.

At the same time this war diary was penned, trench-life was very much the norm and the fighting patterns were getting into a groove. I've heard WW1 referred to as a 'War of Attrition'. This is a strategic concept, which states that to win a war your enemy must be worn down to the point of collapse by continuous losses in personnel and material. I see this as basically: The enemy attacks you. They kill as many of you as possible. You then counter attack. You kill as many of the enemy as you can. Both sides replace casualties and then one side starts the attack-kill process again.

Men, weapons, horses and supplies were constantly being poured into one end of the British lines and dead people, men with horrific injuries and dead animals were coming out of the other end. It's pitiful to think that as well as the human death-toll almost 500,000 horses were lost during this conflict. When I first started reading about the war I had absolutely no concept of this and I tried to fathom out why they'd need so many horses. But, of course, horses were sometimes the only way to get supplies to the front. Roads were shot to pieces and knee-deep in mud. No vehicles could cross the battlefields in those conditions.

This vicious circle of obliteration continued to steam ahead at full pelt with a relentless, indiscriminate, insatiable appetite. It was at this point, in the midst of the unfathomable, mad machinations of warfare, a spontaneous act of human compassion occurred.

Christmas, the season of goodwill and peace. Yeah, right

I doubt there are too many folks who haven't heard about a 'spanner' that well and truly dropped into 'the works' along the Western Front around about Christmas Day 1914. It's come to be known as 'The Christmas Truce'. There have been numerous books and songs written about it as well as several films made to try to re-create and capture this extraordinary moment in human history. Most people will, of course, associate it with British and German soldiers playing football in no-man's-land. It was much more than that. This unplanned, spontaneous activity is well documented and took place at several spots along the fighting lines. I've often wondered how soldiers who were swopping heavy artillery, bullets, grenades and knocking seven bells out of each other one minute, were, the next minute, swopping addresses, souvenirs and socialising. And yes, some did go to the extent of booting a 'caser' round on a make-shift pitch in no-man's-land. Well they say truth is stranger than fiction.

In thinking how it could have happened I can only surmise that because it was winter-time and therefore dark and cold it would seem a hopeless situation. With no end in sight the soldiers would have been missing home comforts and their loved ones. The catalyst for sure would have been the fact that it was the 'season of peace and goodwill to all men'. Christmas affects people in many different ways. For me it generally gets me thinking about Christmas's past, family, decorations, food, snow and happy times. Most recollections of the truce state that it only took a little conversation across no-man's-land, some carol singing and finally one brave soul to actually step out over the parapet of the trench to temporarily halt hostilities. Several recollections state that, at first, each side called a nervous cease-fire just so they could collect their dead from out in no-man's-land. This then escalated into full-on meetings between the two opposing front lines. It's amazing to think of it, really, and to be involved must have been quite literally surreal. Imagine meeting, face to face, with someone who may have actually killed someone standing next to you only a few days earlier.

Harry Hackett, the Black Country Grenadier, was right in the middle of all of this. He experienced this exclusive act up very close and very personal. On Boxing Day 1914 where the official war diary clearly states that his Battalion '...Stood to arms about midnight owing to supposed night attack by the Germans.' Harry met some of these Germans.

Can you imagine what it must have been like actually meeting your enemy face to face? After months of fighting, faceless drones, hoards of impersonal grey figures of hate, you now had the opportunity to communicate as God intended, man to man. You would see their tired faces, their weary eyes, the detail of their battered war-worn uniforms, their breath in the winter air and the now empty hands that yesterday had been pulling triggers and throwing bombs.

In the midst of this, for a split second, maybe you could sense that you were 'perhaps the same'. You were men who were united by location, situation and the camaraderie of war. For that moment, sharing each other's space, you were brothers bonded by circumstance. Your faces reciprocating a contrasting, senseless reflection. Almost like looking at yourself.

We know Harry was caught up in this because he told us. He sent 'that' postcard from the trenches to his beloved Olive explaining that he'd met with the enemy in no-man's-land and, for whatever reason, had the presence of mind to obtain the names and addresses of two of the German soldiers he'd obviously spent time with.

The postcard is plain and simple. On one side it has Olive's address in London along with a half-penny stamp. On the other side it has the usual red Censor's mark and a black Post Office stamp with the letters 'JA 9 15' for January 9th 1915. To the left it has the message to Olive and on the right it has the names of two German soldiers. One name and address is very clear and reads:

> *Rudolf Mausolff*
>
> *Bad Pyrmont*
>
> *(Waldeck)*

The other name is unfortunately obscured by the Post Office stamp but it is possible to make out that the first name is Ernst and that the address contains a location of Bielfeld.

It took quite some time to find anything at all about either soldier but after some considerable detective work I managed to find a single reference to R. Mausolff. He is remembered on a war memorial in Bad Pyrmont, the town stated on Harry's postcard. With some additional expert help it was also established that Rudolf and Ernst were probably with either the 15th Prinz Friedrich der Niederlände or 55th Graf Bülow von Dennewitz Infantry Regiments. Together, these two formed the 26th Infantry Brigade of the 13th Westphalian Infantry Division, stationed in Detmold, halfway between Bielfeld and Pyrmont.

I've often wondered if somewhere in Germany there is someone related to either of these two soldiers. Who knows? Maybe, one day, we will find out. It would be quite special to link our families across Europe to this meeting that happened almost 100 years ago.

There's a great book that I read, when trying to find out more about what happened at this time, simply called 'Christmas Truce' by Malcolm Brown and Shirley Seaton. Harry's 1st Battalion Grenadier Guards are mentioned in it several times. There is a particular reference to a note Lieutenant Colonel Fisher-Rowe wrote to his wife on 27 December 1914 after they had relieved the 2nd Scots Guards somewhere along the Sailly-Fromelles road in Northern France, which says:

> *They (the Germans) wanted to play the Kiddies (2nd Scots Guards) at football yesterday but the Kiddies couldn't supply the ball'.*

This reference obviously confirms that football, anything but fighting, was on the soldiers' minds at the time. Fisher-Rowe also wrote:

> *'We are all very peaceful they (the Germans) say they want the truce to go on till after the New Year and I am sure I have no objection. A rest from bullets will be a distinct change'.*

He then, regrettably, reports to his wife that from 5 January:

> *'...things are back to normal'.*

On reflection this Christmas Truce was an absolutely mind-blowing episode. To think that a relative of mine was actively involved in this historic moment. Remarkable! I feel extremely proud and very honoured. In fact, holding the original postcard in my hands, and realising Harry was as close to it when he wrote it as I am now, makes me connect with the whole thing in a really tangible way. It's very hard to explain but that's just me, I suppose.

'The short visit home'

A short Black Country conversation

"Owbin ya mi mon? I bay sid yer fer yonks"

"I bin ova theyar fightin aye I, and I bay doin' ter good bloke"

"Ow come?"

"On jus come back frum tha frunt aye I. W'een ad a good thraypin off the Bosch an all?"

"Wan ya dun ter yer fairce mi mon?"

"We waz in a scrap an a shell cum ova as big as a bonk 'oss. I gorrit a cockaver. I wan lucky though it neely took mi yed off"

"Am yo finished wi fightin now then chap?"

"No chonce. I gorruw goo back as soon as this un's eeled. Thayme short on blokes owt theyar, thay naydes all th'elp thay con get"

"It doe sarnd ter good mate"

"It aye mate, it's murder mate"

"Lord elp ya mi mon"

"Ta chap...an do us a faver will ya...pray for us mate"

"Wi bin me owd taerter, dow thee werrit abart that'

It was OK for those back in Blighty…wasn't it?

Normal life, or as near to normal as it could be when all the young men of the country were off risking life and limb abroad, bumbled on back in England (or 'Blighty' as our troops would call it). During his few return trips back home on leave Harry had the time to meet with and eventually marry his sweetheart. On 9 February 1916 he had 'tied the knot' with Olive Doretta Cook, in the Dudley Register Office, just a few miles up the road from the family home in Old Hill. Olive was from Bodinnick, near Fowey in Cornwall but working as a domestic servant in London where she must have met Harry. Her address on their marriage certificate is stated as 11 Westmoreland Street, Pimlico, London. It's a beautiful area of London and quite classy. The houses are classic white-painted, terraced buildings. Number 11 still exists today. It is a stone's throw from the Thames and about a mile from Buckingham Palace. It's also very close to Wellington and Chelsea Barracks where the Grenadiers stayed when on duty in London, so I'd imagine this is how they met in 1912. They both worked in the same neck of the woods.

There was no texting, email, Facebook or Twitter back then (however did they cope!). Information must have travelled extremely slowly by present day standards. Nevertheless the war-time postal service was efficient and very reliable. News would have been precious and I guess the main outlets would have been newspapers, word of mouth and of course letters. Incoming and outgoing mail was seen as an absolute necessity to our troops in order to maintain contact and uphold morale. Correspondence routes and regular deliveries to each soldier, even in the trenches, were seen as especially high priority. It wasn't just letters that loved ones would post to the trenches but packages too. They would contain more or less anything. You name it, people posted it. I've read accounts of things like tinned food, jam, socks, gloves and even the less obvious like birthday cakes. All packed with care and posted in England to be delivered to a loved one at an address no more than a hole in a mud wall known as a dug-out. Olive regularly sent parcels to Harry 'at the front' and he often acknowledged and thanked her for them in his letters;

"1st January 1915...I received your parcel today for which I thank you very much. The helmet [knitted balaclava] *will come in very useful during these cold nights...mail comes in almost every day now...Do not trouble to send me any more* [cigarettes] *as I have now got plenty to last me for a long time but if you like you might send a couple of pair of those socks and also one or two of those handkerchiefs you said you were making, that is if you don't feel tired when you receive this letter".*

"29 January 1915...I was very grateful for those cakes as I could not eat hardly for two days but I managed the cakes alright, I have been under the Medical Officer for these last two days, but I am now getting all right again".

Later in the year on Guy Fawkes Night 1915, Harry reports on the state of a parcel that must've had a bit of a rough ride on the way;

"My Dearest Olive. I received your parcel alright yesterday afternoon...mine was knocked about a bit, the cake was all smashed up and that carbolic soap you put in got mixed up with the sandwiches somehow and made the cake taste of soap...thank you very much for the socks...and the tea and sugar will come in alright when we go into the trenches again next week as sometimes we get chance to make a small fire...".

On 11 December 1915 he also received;

"...a very large parcel of different things', from the Salvation Army Officer at Cradley Heath [near Harry's home town of Old Hill] *which was subscribed for by some of my old pals...we go into the trenches tomorrow and I can hardly carry it all..."*

Soldiers would generally return home to England on a regular basis. They would be either on leave or, of course, the badly injured who would spend time convalescing before being returned to the front. There would also be the very badly injured, who would be excluded from fighting, being sent home for good. Soldiers would be pretty visible on the streets of most, if not all, British towns. My nan recalls seeing soldiers around when she was very young. She was born in February 1914 and she told me a tale once of visiting her grannie's house in Old Hill. She vividly remembers seeing one of her uncles in a soldier's uniform. I suppose this could possibly have been Harry or his brother Samuel home on leave. They used to get the kids to run errands for them to get cigarettes from the local shop in return for a penny that they could spend on sweets. She says they used to bring the cigarettes one at a time in the hope of being given more pennies.

I doubt anyone at home could really understand what these returning lads had been through and there are many accounts of soldiers not wanting to discuss details. I suppose they just wanted to forget for the few days they were home and to escape from the constant noise, uncertainty, doom and gloom. In another letter dated 12 February 1915 Harry again touches on the situations and trials he was facing;

"My Dearest Olive. I am writing this letter to give to one of my friends, who is going on leave today, to post in England as I thought I may be able to put a little more news in it without it being censored...I could have come [home] *today Thursday but I have let this Sergeant who is posting the letter go in my place as he has got his wife very bad in bed after confinement and the child has since died...I must say the weather is quite fine out here now to what we have been having although it is rather cold at night. The place we are at now is called Sailly-Sur-La-Lys just on the left of La-Basse and we have been here since the beginning of last December. It has not been quite so hard since being here but before then it was awful as we were in that big affair at Ypres when we lost about 28 Officers and 800 NCO and men out of our battalion and I think when we had finished there was 1 Officer and 190 NCO and men left. I escaped it by the skin of my teeth many a time. I thought many a day was going to be my last as we had over seventy thousand Germans against our Division which was about twenty thousand strong. But I think we have got the upper hand of them now although they will take a lot of beating...I am writing this letter in a house where the Crown Prince of Bavaria stopped when the Germans were here..."*

I have read the letter that the above excerpt is from many, many times. It gives me a real sense of what Harry was thinking and really brings home some of the realities of war and shows some of the kindness and character of Harry. As you will see he graciously allowed someone he thought had a much greater need than he did, to escape home for a few days. Also, of course, it outlines his location in Northern France as he circumvented the strict censor policy by getting a pal to 'smuggle' the letter home. And in an open, honest and chilling way he states how close, and how often, he faced death or injury.

The Crown Prince, by the way, was one of the most senior German chiefs and was considered by some to have been one of the best Royal Commanders in the Imperial German Army. The Prince, whose full title was the rather grandiose, His Royal Highness Rupprecht Maria Luitpold Ferdinand, Crown Prince of Bavaria, Duke of Bavaria, of Franconia and in Swabia, Count Palatine of the Rhine, was also one of the first German Generals to come to the conclusion, towards the end of 1917, that the war could not be won.

A month later and Harry and his battalion are still fighting. In a letter dated 16 March 1915 he explains why he hasn't been able to write to Olive in over a week;

"My Dearest Olive. As I have now an hour to spare after roughing it for a bit for the last week I will write you a few more lines...I am sorry I was unable to write last week as there has been another big battle here in which there has been a lot of lives lost again on both sides. I can hardly explain my feelings Olive...It is a great consolation to me to know there is someone who is praying for my guidance..."

24 March 1915 "...I am as well as can be under the circumstances...I have been thinking this last day or two about the last 3 years what a lot has happened little did either of us think twelve months ago this war would be on and whilst I am only one out of thousands out here under the same circumstances I do not think there is anyone who has felt the pinch of being parted more than what I have...I expect you have heard me talk about those other two Sergeants who were range-takers with me. Well I am sorry to say they have now both been killed. I also feel sorry for those they have left behind as I know they were both on the point of getting married and both girls are in Service at South Kensington".

Harry obviously senses the similarities of the two soldier's positions as he, too, is a Sergeant and his girlfriend Olive is in Service in and around South Kensington. He must have felt extremely fortunate but at the same time worried whether he might meet the same fate.

Samuel Hackett – Harry's little brother

You may have spotted the reference to Samuel earlier. He was Harry's younger brother and he also served in the Great War. When he enlisted his record states that he was: '5 foot 4 and a quarter of an inch tall and of fair complexion'. His age is stated on his sign-up papers as 'nineteen years and one month'. However, his actual age at the time, according to the 1911 Census, would have been just sixteen. This is classic 'lied about his age to join up' war-time stuff and not uncommon. He was assigned to the local Worcestershire Regiment with the 7th Battalion and, by all accounts Samuel Hackett, was a bit of a handful. More on that subject later. First, let's just get a feel for Sam's war.

Sam arrived in France in May 1917 and on 10 June he was posted to the 4th Worcestershire Regiment. Two days later he joined the Battalion 'in the field'. This means close to where the action was. At some point in the spring the 4th Battalion were involved in the Battle of Arras. They then found themselves in the Ypres Salient (remember, not a nice place to be for a British soldier) where they remained until mid-October 1917.

On 9 October Sam's Service record states that he was 'Wounded in action'. He was moved first to 56 General Hospital in Etaples, France and then returned home aboard the hospital ship 'Ville de Liege'. The injury was some kind of gash to the left shoulder caused by shrapnel and he stayed in Number 2 Hospital, Canterbury for twenty-four days. He was then moved through the rehabilitation system as follows. Admitted to the Military Hospital, Preston Hall, Aylesford. Discharged and moved to Southern Command Depot, Ballyvonare Camp in Buttevant, County Cork.

Once fully recovered he was returned to the 4th Worcestershire Regiment. He embarked at Folkestone and disembarked at Boulogne on 5 April 1918. The next day he was moved to Etaples. On 8 April he was 'back in the field' with the 1/7th Worcestershire Regiment. Within six days he was back in hospital. On 15 May, at the 150 Field Ambulance, (note a Field Ambulance was a mobile front line medical unit it was not a vehicle), his casualty record indicates him as having 'P.U.O.' At first glance I had absolutely no idea what these three letters stood for. A few days later I was able to devote a few hours to study and found that they stood for: Pyrexia of Unknown Origin also known as F.U.O. or Fever of Unknown Origin. To you and me this would have been known as Trench Fever, a particularly painful disease that began suddenly with severe pain followed by high fever. P.U.O. was quite an unusual condition and almost exclusive to WW1 soldiers. Apparently it died out after the war. This new disease meant men would need to be kept well away from the trenches. It could take anything up to twelve weeks to recover.

Due to this illness, Sam was again on his way back to England via 16 General Hospital at Le Treport, on the French coast. He was then finally transferred home aboard the hospital ship 'St David'.

Sam's last sickness report was from Horton War Hospital in Epsom on 1 June 1918 records clearly, 'Trench Fever'. With an annotation of, 'Three weeks leg pains and fever. Heart and lungs nil'.

After spending time once again going through the process of recovery, he is posted to 7th Reserve Unit, Sutton Coldfield returning to France ten days before the end of the war. On 10 March 1919 Sam finally leaves the army after serving 3 years 290 days.

This short overview of Sam is, unfortunately, only one side of the coin.

Whilst these apparently normal activities 'fighting in trenches, getting injured and subsequent recoveries', were taking place there was a parallel sub-plot in progress.

An official Army service records details events such as postings or transfers, injuries, promotions, and in some rare cases, offences. I've covered Sam's postings, transfers and injuries. There are no promotions. So that only leaves one other category to cover. The majority of Sam's paperwork reads more like a mini military criminal record. It's peppered with hand-written, dated and signed annotations. Alas they are not commendations, promotions or acts of bravery in the field. The vast majority of entries are offences 'committed whilst serving'.

At first Sam appears to be very willing to be a soldier and get involved. He even lied about his age so that he could enlist. But his record shows no less than twelve separate offences. They have a common thread of insubordination, rebelliousness or defiance; call it what you will. Here they are, by date of offence. Please note for clarification I've amended some of the structure and spellings from the original hand-written documentation.

23 April 1916 - Deprived 7 days pay for 'Overstaying his pass from 9pm till 9pm, 24 hours' at Windmill Hill Camp, Salisbury Plain.

29 October 1916 - Given 21 days detention for (i) Not complying with an order. (ii) Insolence to an NCO at Cheltenham. Deprived 5 days pay.

1 December 1916 - 'Dirty rifle on parade' at Cheltenham, awarded 2 days confined to barracks.

15 December 1916 - 'Absent from parade 7am', at Cheltenham, awarded 2 days confined to barracks.

2 January 1917 – 'Absent from parade 7am', at Cheltenham, awarded 3 days confined to barracks.

27 February 1917 – 'Dirty equipment on 8:15am parade', awarded 3 days confined to barracks.

17 September 1917 - (i) Inattention on Commanding Officer on parade. (ii) Being improperly dressed on parade. Whilst in the field. (This means when on active duty, possibly in the trenches) Awarded 7 days Confined to barracks.

29 March 1918 - 'Insolence to an NCO, awarded 5 days Confined to barracks'. Whilst at Blythe.

27 July 1918 - 'Overstaying his special pass' whilst at Sutton Coldfield, awarded 3 days confined to barracks and forfeited 1 day's pay.

13 September 1918 - 'Overstaying his pass from Tattoo 9:38pm until 11:20pm on 14 Sept 1918 (25 hrs 10 mins)'. Whilst at Blyth, punishment was stated as 'Admonished' awarded 3 days confined to barracks and forfeited 1 day's pay

22 October 1918 - 'Absent from Tattoo 9:30am and remaining absent until found in his hut at reveille'. Whilst at Blythe. Awarded 14 days confined to barracks. Also forfeited 1 day's pay.

2 January 1919 - Awarded (F.P. No 1) for 'Hesitating to comply with an order by his Commanding Officer'. Whilst in the Field.

I know there's a lot to discuss here but let's just focus on that last statement for a while.

F.P. No 1 or Field Punishment Number 1. This sentence was also referred to by our troops as 'crucifixion' which might give you a clue regarding what it resembled. The punishment as decreed by the British Army involved the offender being hand-cuffed, shackled in leg-irons and bound upright to a fixed object such as a cross-shaped structure or a cartwheel. They would remain fixed in this position for up to two hours a day, for several days on end.

The 1914 Manual of Military Law specifically stated that Field Punishment No. 1 'should not be applied in such a way as to cause physical harm'. However in practice abuses were commonplace. Accounts I've come across detail occurrences of prisoners being deliberately placed in stress positions such as ensuring their feet were not fully touching the ground. Occasionally it was also acceptable to position these men in a place that was within range of enemy shell-fire. It was an extremely uncomfortable, embarrassing public display of discipline. The punishment was meant to deter the culprit from wandering off the straight and narrow again as well as discourage onlookers from even thinking of doing the same. In addition to 'crucifixion' the soldier in question was also subjected to hard labour and loss of pay just to put a 'topper' on it.

Sam's offence was recorded as the day after New Year's day 1919, so he would have been lashed to something like a gun carriage, outdoors, in what would have been typical freezing, winter conditions. He would have suffered this for two hours a day for twenty-eight days as detailed in the sentence. It's also worth noting that this offence took place well after the war had ended. Even without the threat of having to fight Germans in the terrible conditions of the trenches, he was still resisting military authority.

F.P. 1 or simply 'No 1' as it was called was first introduced in 1881 following the abolition of flogging. It was eventually abolished in 1923.

The list of Sam's offences almost read like a stereotypical WW1 soldier who lies about his age in order to join the 'glorious' war but who then can't cope with the orders, rules and regulations. Some of the offences are almost comical; dirty rifle, improperly dressed, back chatting officers and over staying his pass while out on the town. He was generally punished with loss of pay and confined to barracks. I thought I'd do a little digging as 'confined to barracks' sounds a little 'light' in the punishment department. I imagined Sam, feet-up, lying on his bed in the barracks maybe sucking on a 'roll-up', reading the newspaper or snoozing. But after asking my father-in-law Sid Hawkins (who was himself confined to barracks during his service after WW2) what it was like, he said, 'It was definitely nothing like that at all'. Confined to barracks meant some hard labour duties, being called up for uniform and kit inspection at a moment's notice and the like. He himself was once made to cut the lawn outside the barracks with a pair of scissors! I should point out also that he was only punished because following an inspection, after being asked to clean out the barrack room, a Sergeant had detected 'dust on the coals' in the coal bucket!

Sam's 'crime' was of course a little more 'Premier League' than this. They didn't dish out punishment like this unless someone seriously crossed the line. FP No 1 is a whisker away from being shot at dawn. It is serious stuff. Sam's was for 'Hesitating to comply with an order whilst in the field'. We can only surmise what he might or might not have refused to comply with. The most important principal in the army at the time was (and is) 'Never refuse an order'.

Who knows what Sam was going through during his WW1? He'd lied in order to sign up. Perhaps he wanted to follow in his big 'hero-brother' Harry's footsteps. Maybe it was peer pressure or he, like lots of teenagers, just wanted to get involved and get some action. Possibly when he arrived at the Regimental Depot for training he just couldn't cope with the shock to the system that army orders, hard work, discipline and routine brings. Maybe he just couldn't cope with going over the top and witnessing carnage and fear. After all he would only have been seventeen or eighteen years old while he was in the trenches, killing people. The offences are clear, unquestionable and plentiful.

So while Sam is contending with punishment, reprimands as well as his unfortunate physical injuries. Harry is taking part in battle after battle, maintaining an unblemished record with promotion after promotion and he finds time to correspond with his sweetheart, get married and even start a family.

Back to our Harry

Occasionally soldiers were 'attached' to other battalions and during May 1915 Harry highlighted this annotating his usual address on the top of his letters with 'Attached to 55th Company Royal Engineers'. Whilst serving with them on 7 May he wrote;

"…tomorrow we are for it again you will know what I mean when you read this letter as I expect there will be something in the papers about it by the time this reaches you. I do not think I will be able to stick it much longer, there has been three sergeants of my Company invalided home this week but then I expect they know that I am half done for and being practically the only Sergeant out here who came out at the kick off makes it worse for me…we have just been given orders to pack up at once so I'll guess there's something on, a few more lives going West I expect still we must cheer up and look on the bright side it's all for King and Country".

Sixteen days later from 4th Company, 1st Battalion Grenadier Guards he comments on the 'latest battle';

"My Dearest Olive. You must please excuse me once again for keeping you waiting so long for a line as I expect you have seen in the papers all about this latest battle which I think has been more of a success than the last one. I expect you remember me writing about a fortnight ago and telling you there was another one coming off, well that one was a failure in one way and since then we have been to a different part of the line and had another go which has proved more successful although we have had a few casualties again but I am pleased to say that I have come through once again alright".

"Well Dearest I think this is about all I can write tonight as I feel a bit down-hearted somehow since reading your letter it has made me think a bit

but I am pleased to say all is well so will close. With truest love, from yours only, Harry xxx".

In July and August 1915 Harry was fortunate to have some well-deserved rest when his company was posted to 'the country'. He reports;

"I am quite well myself and could do with stopping in this place for a month or two it is like living in heaven…"

"We are away from the firing line awaiting to be formed into our new Division. It is going to be called the First Guards Division and our Battalion is in the Third Brigade…I think it will be worse now the Guards are together as they expect such a lot from us. We were inspected yesterday by the President of France, Lord Kitchener and Sir John French so we can guess what is coming off…I think it is hard-lines for us who have been out all the winter as we are expected to be just as fit as those who have only just come out, and I know I am not half so fit as I was twelve months ago…hope I shall be with you again before long, remember me to all and hope you are still enjoying your holidays".

The heavenly place Harry referred to was obviously in stark contrast to his considerable time spent in the firing line. In a later note he states the place as being Wizernes in Northern France. The visit from the 'big-wigs' also signified inspection before a significant 'push' or fracas with the enemy. His next letter dated 21 October 1915 confirms this quite clearly;

"…we have been having a warm time of it and although I have been amongst some of the thickest of the recent fighting I am pleased to say I have pulled through alright. It is not very often I mention in a letter, as you know, much about what has happened out here but I can tell you Dear Olive it is a miracle how I did get through this time. Although I cannot go through the details of the fighting it will ever live in my memory. We are now for a day or two's rest the first since this great battle began, so you can guess how welcome it is. I have not wrote for so long and no doubt by the time you get this letter we shall be in the trenches again…Thank you for the parcel you sent, it came one night as we were just going into the trenches but managed to carry it along with me…"

He finishes with;

"...hope I have not got to spend another winter out here, have now had quite enough having been at it over twelve months now, still must hope for the best..."

Ten days later it seems his hope of a return home before winter were very unlikely;

"...I expected at one time to be sent home for winter, but have now given up all hope...I should very much like to be with you on your 21st birthday which will shortly be here [18 December]. I don't know why but I have been thinking about that for a long time. I shall never forget last year's as it was on that day there was a charge made by the Scots Guards and they lost a few good men. We also had a rough time getting into the trenches as they were half full of water and got wet through..."

In the same letter he also explains to Olive a very close call;

"...a shell burst within two yards of me and never hardly touched me but smashed my rifle. I have had some very narrow escapes before but I think that is about the nearest one".

He ends his letter with;

"..in about two hours' time I shall be in the trenches again...From your loving boy, Harry xxx".

His extended stint 'up at the sharp end' continues and on 15 November 1915 he again mentions his time in the trenches and hints that he is due to visit the very same ones he was fighting in almost twelve months earlier. He also comments on the weather which seems to be causing concerns and also pains in his legs;

"...tomorrow we go in the trenches again...I suppose we shall find a change in them this time as it has rained almost every day out here this last fortnight and I know what a state they were in last winter. Still I suppose we shall have to go through it but I hardly think I shall last out this winter the same as I did last as my legs are already beginning to ache at the first bit of damp weather. I sometimes wish they would send me to hospital for about a couple of months just to buck me up a bit as you know I am just about half and

half, if you understand what I mean. Not quite bad enough to be sent out of it and yet am not fit to stop here".

Four days later, the weather is starting to deteriorate as winter sets in. He also receives some bad news from home;

"My own Dearest Olive. I received the cardigan you sent alright yesterday…it will come in alright as the weather is getting extremely cold now especially at night time but we are being provided with as much as possible with things to keep us warm. We came out of the trenches again last night…they are not going to let us stop in the trenches for more than two day's at a time now the weather is getting so bad and it's a good job too…". *"I have received a letter from home and they tell me that the young fellow that my cousin Ruth Brettle married has been killed…".* *"..our band the Grenadiers are giving a concert this afternoon so will close for this time. With fondest and best love from your loving boy, Harry xxx".*

This was his final letter of 1915 apart from a hand-made birthday card he must have made whilst in the trenches. It was decorated with tiny, colourful bows and signed 'From your sweetheart Harry'. The next letter dated 28 February 1916 does not open with Harry's usual 'To my Dearest Olive' but 'My Own Darling Wife'. Harry had managed to have some home-leave and was now a married man. Unfortunately his opening paragraph reveals some worrying news;

"I came out of hospital on Friday last and am back with my Battalion again and am pleased to say they are not going in the trenches for a day or two so it will give me time to get settled down again…"

It sounds as if he received an injury to his leg or foot as he appeared a little unsteady on his feet;

"…some of them here [his fellow soldiers] *wanted to know if I was drunk, I shall have to show you the mark it has left when I come back…I received congratulations from my Company Officers this morning and they welcomed me back…my hands and feet are now almost frozen as it is bitter cold out here just now and the barn we are sleeping in is almost as bad as living in the open…".*

There is then a huge gap of over two years between this and his next letter. The time span concurs with Harry's service record and it seems he returned to England on 29 March 1916, more than likely due to a further injury.

Just prior to his return Harry and the rest of the 1st Battalion Grenadier Guards had a short break from the front and were allowed two day's rest, around 24 March 1916, in the delightfully named Belgian town of Poperinge. 'Pops', as it was known to our British soldiers, must have been a welcome oasis of normality to them. It was located eight miles to the west of Ypres and, remember, just two miles further east was the mayhem of the Ypres Salient. Poperinge was far enough behind the troubles to allow our soldiers, or 'Tommies' as they were known, to sit back and relax. 'Pops' is a quiet, small, typical Flemish village with a spacious town square, it was also home to Toc H. No, that wasn't a typo. Toc H is what the troops called the unique Talbot House.

The British army practically commandeered the entire town to accommodate the life and soul of its living, breathing, fighting machine. 'Pops' became the twenty-four hour, seven days a week 'Principality of Tommy'. To give you an idea of the scale of what it had to cope with, by 1917 a quarter of a million British soldiers were sheltered there.

In December 1915, near the centre of this busy mini-city, a Chaplain by the name of Philip (Tubby) Clayton opened what he called a 'soldiers' house'. A large 18th Century hop merchant's house on one of the main streets was converted into an 'Every Man's Club'. It was distinctive in as much as all soldiers were welcome, regardless of rank. Back in the day, the lower ranks didn't mix with officers. It wasn't the done thing. Toc H was specifically brought into being to overcome this so that men could simply relax and enjoy each other's company in the midst of the stress, bloodshed and madness. There they could enjoy mugs of tea, warmth, music or find some peace and quiet to read a book, there was also a chapel in the loft and in latter years a small Concert Hall.

On the suggestion of a senior Colonel the house was named 'Talbot House'. This was intended to specifically commemorate a chap by the name of Gilbert Talbot, who was killed in action on 30 July 1915. Gilbert was to signify and symbolise the sacrifice of our young men, also known as the 'golden generation'.

For the next three years Talbot House provided our soldiers with an alternative to the unsurprisingly 'debauched' recreational life found elsewhere in numerous towns behind the lines. With the pressures and stresses of First World War combat it would be negligent to consider that the usual vices of alcohol and women were not an unusual feature of anywhere our troops were expected to chill out.

With this backdrop it's heartening to think that for hundreds of thousands of our young men, this place became 'a home from home'. Anecdotes from numerous Toc H visitors always mentioned that there they found a little bit of the sparse, war-time commodities of humanity, rest and peace.

After this brief respite in 'Pops', Harry was transferred to the 5th (Reserve) Battalion Grenadier Guards and on 29 March 1916 returned to England. From the records it appears that he spent some time recovering from an injury at a Manor House that had been requisitioned for hospital-work, based in Dorchester, Dorset. It is not known how Harry was injured, but having to return to England must have meant that he needed serious medical treatment and recuperation. Once he recovered he would have returned to Caterham, Surrey the Grenadier Guards depot he'd trained at. Some fourteen months later on 16 May 1917 while still stationed in England, Harry was promoted from Sergeant to the rank of Acting Company Quartermaster Sergeant. The CQMS is a Non-Commissioned Officer (NCO) in a company and the role serves as deputy to the Company Sergeant Major and is the second most senior NCO in the company. It's a pretty senior rank in any regiment requiring responsibility for supplies. Without careful management of these an Army becomes impotent.

Harry continued his military career based in England at Little Sparta. That is until things started to get extremely desperate for the British Army in and around an area known as the Lys in Northern France.

Things were about to change.

On 6 April 1918, for some unknown reason, Harry relinquished his rank of Acting Quartermaster Sergeant and reverted back to Sergeant. He was about to return to the front.

Some 'Huge Ass' battle in The Somme

If you know a little about the First World War you will quite probably be aware of the phrase 'The Somme' that gets bandied about. The Somme is an area around a river of the same name in France about 100 miles north of Paris. A critical, huge 'mother of a battle' was fought here, more or less right in the middle of the four and a bit year Great War. This particular battle had a significant effect on the overall casualty figures and has come to epitomise the futility of trench warfare and to make controversial the Commanders in charge of our forces. So what was this battle all about and why was it fought at all?

In essence the battle was directly aimed at supporting the French army who had been suffering horrendously for months at Verdun, about 160 miles to the east of Paris. After all, this was predominantly a French and Belgian war. We, the British, weren't defending British territory; we were supporting our close political friends and allies. At Verdun the French forces had been on the receiving end of a severe 'thumping'. They were haemorrhaging men and resources at a monstrous rate. Check out the following numbers. During the ten-month Battle of Verdun, from 21 February to 18 December 1916, there were, on average, 30,000 deaths every single day. A shocking figure by any stretch! The battle lasted for 300 days and 300 nights. 26 million bombs dropped by the opposing artillery units. That's six bombs for every square metre of the battlefield.

It is well worth noting and acknowledging the incredible sacrifice the French army made in defence of their homeland. It's also important to remember that many nations, including Britain and her Commonwealth, stood shoulder to shoulder with France and Belgium during the Great War. There are thousands of graves scattered along the length and breadth of what was the Western Front to mark where Canadian, Australian, Newfoundland, Portuguese, New Zealand, Indian and South African soldiers fought and died. These Allied Forces along with France and Belgium were all focussed on defeating the

German invaders. Verdun was a key killing ground for the French and Germans. France lost almost 400,000 men defending it. Germany lost about the same. 300,000 bodies were never recovered. Verdun now remembers these men at the Douaumont Ossuary site. Its imposing forty-six metre high tower offers panoramic views over the surrounding ex-battlefields. The Ossuary, which is the term used for somewhere that houses skeletal remains, also houses the remains of 130,000 unidentified soldiers. These 'bones' are all clearly visible through purposefully placed windows. This may sound ghoulish or voyeuristic but when you consider this in the context of what Verdun stands for, it's a pragmatic way of paying respect without hiding away the realities and human costs.

Consequently, in 1916, in order to relieve the French from this 'black-hole' which consumed soldiers at an alarming rate, the Allied High Command devised a plan. This was to attack the Germans in The Somme some 170 kilometres North West of Verdun. This would mean that the German army would need to respond and move a great deal of their men away from the Verdun battlefield thus relieving the long-suffering French. Relieving pressure on the French Army was crucial and was the first main objective of the Somme offensive. The second and third objectives were, simple: Slaughter as many enemy soldiers and create as much disorder, destruction and devastation as possible for the Germans. Great Wars are 'great' aren't they?

You may find this hard to believe but General Foch, the man in charge of the entire French Army, believed that the planned attack in the Somme by the joint armies would achieve little. You might then think, 'Durr!, so why bother doing it and sacrificing so many lives?' There's no answer to this and unfortunately the army's political masters in London and Paris ignored any concerns and ordered the battle to take place as planned.

The main 'big push' was preceded by the British bombarding the entire twenty-five miles of German front–line trenches for seven days around the clock. 1.7 million shells were launched during this onslaught. The thinking was that this vast, concentrated firepower would just flatten the enemy troops, their equipment and also smash the 'rats-nest' of barbed wire protecting the German front-lines. It was an absolutely critical point that this deadly 'wire' (a feature of all the trenches on the Western Front and anything up to several metres deep) was cut or destroyed. This would allow our infantry to march straight through it once the attack started without being held up trying to negotiate the barbed wire entanglements and ending up as sitting ducks for the 'rabid' German machine-guns.

There are no end of outstanding books that describe the Battle of the Somme in greater detail than I could ever hope to achieve. So I will just summarise what could be a huge narrative by means of my modest, 'top five dummy's guide' which follows:

Clanger 1: The preliminary seven-day artillery bombardment unfortunately had the associated effect of well and truly letting the enemy know that 'something big was about to go down'. Not wanting to 'spoil the party' the German Army had plenty of time to 'tool up' and get ready to respond at a moment's notice.

Clanger 2: The attack on the line near Beaumont Hamel was to be co-ordinated and initiated by the ignition of a huge bomb, (that actually left a crater twenty-two metres deep and three hundred metres wide), known as the Hawthorn Mine. But it went off a full ten minutes before the agreed zero-hour (7:30am) when the lads were due to hop 'over the top'. Ten minutes was plenty of time for the Germans to recover from the initial, 'What the **** was that!', get to their posts and man their machine-guns.

Clanger 3: The German dugouts were not just regular 'head-height' trenches, but extremely well-constructed, several metres deep and very seriously fortified. The men were simply able to shelter in their underground bunkers in relative safety until it went quiet and they spotted our infantry walking (note, our men were under strict orders not to run that day), towards their awaiting machine-gun nests.

Clanger 4: The 1.7 million shells that showered down over seven days and nights had done a fantastic job of churning up the ground in front of the enemy trenches. The ground was so badly clobbered that it was a nightmare trying to walk across cross no-man's-land whilst at the same time trying to avoid being spotted and picked-off by the defenders. Also every soldier had to negotiate this bomb-site carrying a combined weight of 27 kilograms of kit on their backs. Or the equivalent weight of a fully grown Golden Retriever.

Clanger 5: Thousands of British shells failed to explode leaving some areas of the German defences virtually in 'mint condition'. Some reports I've seen reckon that one in every three of our shells was 'dud'.

It gets worse.

Twenty-four hours after the 'whistle was blown' on 1 July 1916 to signal our lads to go 'over the top' 20,000 British Soldiers lay dead. What's more, there were a further 60,000 who were wounded and incapable of continuing the fight.

The Battle of The Somme was, and still is, the British Military's greatest ever loss of life in a single day. Even that wasn't the end though! When the Somme 'big push' was finally called off on 28 November 1916, more than 450,000 British, 200,000 French and 650,000 German soldiers had met their maker.

So what do you get for 650,000 Allied lives and four months of fighting? Well in this case you get to advance a 'grand total' of five miles. Sums like that just don't add up do they?

Over the years those who led the British campaign have received a lot of criticism for the way the Battle of the Somme was fought. One man's name always crops up and that would be Field Marshall Douglas Haig. War is always messy and unpredictable but the things our lads had to do for King and Country were at times pointless and at the very worst, insane. Don't even get me started on a 'cunning' device to be worn on the backpacks of our advancing troops. These little shiny tin-triangles reflected in the sunlight so that our artillery spotters and commanders, who would have been at least a million miles away in a tree house, could keep an eye on the battle in progress. Thing is, these little triangles worked great when you were advancing towards the enemy. But as soon as the enemy had you on the run and you retreated, they acted like a glowing neon 'Yoo hoo!, Mr German, here I am, please shoot me' sign. Stupid and tragic.

The Battle of The Somme is now ingrained into British history and the military psyche. Several lessons were learned, but at what cost!

The Battle of The Lys is a far less well-known 'fracas'. Nonetheless this battle played its part and was itself at the centre of a decisive phase for both the Allies and the German warmongers. The Lys is a river that runs through Belgium and Northern France. A series of brutal, strategically important battles took place in its vicinity. The majority of the combat I would like to focus on is in or around the town of Hazebrouck because this is where the 4th Battalion Grenadiers and (more importantly for me) where Harry was.

When the going gets tough, you need more toughies

Here's some context setting the scene for the final few days of Harry's short life. When I wrote the words in the previous sentence they seemed very blunt and cold. 'Final', 'days' and 'life' are words that conjure up thoughts of the end of the line, sadness, loss and pain. The abrupt curtailing of what could have been. No one wants to hear these words. They resonate with an inevitable certainty, an unavoidable, unwelcomed end-result, an undesirable, ultimate destination.

A few short years before, Harry had signed up and joined one of the elite fighting forces of his time. He had been involved in combat where he would have been fighting for his life, the life of others and the life of a country. He had experienced the emotions of celebrating a few Christmas's away from home in fear for his life. One Christmas he had even met someone face to face whose job it was to destroy him. They had exchanged names and addresses. Who knows, maybe they agreed to meet after the war was over. He'd been in innumerable battles, perilous situations and gory skirmishes as well as witnessing countless friends fall at his side. As a wounded soldier he'd been sent home to England to recover from an unknown but debilitating injury. He had then returned to what was a non-combat role carrying out duties in his regiment's main London barracks.

Then it was decided, by the military hierarchy, that he and others would be sent back into the firing line.

He would soon be facing the full might of a battle-wise, frenzied, ultra-aggressive German Army who were desperate to fulfil the orders of their Kaiser and 'terminate' anyone or anything in its way. Oh yes, I forgot to add, that whilst based in England on 18 January 1918, Harry had become a father. His son, William Samuel Harry Hackett, was

107

born in London. It's sad to report that it is very highly likely that due to the circumstances of his role and the perilous phase of the war, Harry may have seen very little, if anything, of his new son. This is particularly heart-rending.

On 6 April 1918 Harry's service record shows that he was 're-inserted' back into the jaws of the uninterruptable war to face what was documented as some of the fiercest fighting of the entire campaign. As previously stated, he had reverted to Sergeant at precisely this time. Perhaps Quartermasters were not allowed to join the efforts in the field. Perhaps he requested to join his fellow Grenadiers at the sharp end. Perhaps he had no choice. Who knows? The fact is, he returned to active duty.

Two days later he writes;

"My Own Dearest Wife. At last I am able to drop you a few lines and am pleased to say I have arrived over here quite safe and am now at rest camp. I suppose you heard the noise Saturday night when we went away, we had a good send off at Charing Cross…I do not know nothing definite about what Battalion I am going to but probably it will be the 1st the one I was with before…hope the baby is still getting on alright. I suppose you felt lonely a bit after I went but never mind Dear hope it will not be long before I am back again with you…With my fondest, truest and best love to you and baby. From your loving husband, Harry xxx".

He also adds a few special kisses at the bottom of the letter 'For Baby'.

Unlike his first visit to France four years prior to this, he would know exactly what he and his pals had coming to them. It must have been ultra-stressful. With news of the casualty figures coming back from the front due to these new German assaults, some might be forgiven for entertaining the thought that they were 'dead men walking'.

Quite simply Harry returned to France because at the front 'they were running out of men'. On arrival he was assigned to the 4th Battalion Grenadier Guards who were in the midst of an epic dust up with the German army in The Lys.

Harry's penultimate letter explains that he hasn't moved far since landing. He was still at the rest camp on 11 April 1918. He also sounds pretty comfortable and relaxed;

"I am unable at present to give you any definite address as I am still at the same place as when I wrote last. Well Dear I expect by now you are down in Fowey [Olive's family home in Cornwall] *and I hope you arrived quite safely and baby is still alright. I do not know when I shall move from here but as soon as I am settled I will let you know the address. I must say I have had a nice time so far wouldn't mind sticking here for duration, right on the sea front, the same as where I was in hospital...we have lovely weather so far...I cannot say much more now as you know these letters are censored so will close. Give baby a kiss each night for me...".*

No surrender, no running away, we're British!

In the early months of 1918 the German Army had been making major gains. The British had been suffering increasingly heavy losses and they were about to face the second part of General Ludendorff's strategic plan named Operation Georgette. They sensed the possible death throes of the British Army so decided to pour in men and machinery in an attempt to finish the job for the 'umpteenth' time. The German objective was simple: Take back the city of Ypres. This offensive was what would later become known as the Battle of the Lys. The day after Harry arrived, the German 6th Army began executing the plan. It was 'show-time'.

With the situation turning desperate, Field Marshall Haig the commander of our forces issued his 'Backs To The Wall' order of the day. It contained these key chilling sentences.

'There is no other course open to us but to fight it out! Every position must be held to the last man: there must be no retirement. With our backs to the wall and believing in the justice of our cause, each one of us must fight on to the end'.

Pretty scary stuff to be told basically, fight until you win or you can fight no more. As the battle progressed particularly between the 11 and 14 April, the 4th Battalion Grenadiers were involved in some of the fiercest fighting of the war in which many soldiers carried out Haig's order to the letter.

On 12 April the 4th Grenadiers were ordered forward to take certain key villages in the area in order to strengthen positions and 'shape-up' fighting lines. Before The Guards could get stuck into this task they were robustly attacked and held up by a seriously strong German force. They were desperately in need of reinforcements and a huge Australian Division was ordered up from the rear to support them. This urgently needed help would, of course, take quite some time to arrive. It was a desperate situation and so desperate measures were required. The British Army commanders issued an official order which was hastily prepared and circulated to all the troops. It more or less said, 'No retirement would be allowed without an order in writing, signed by a responsible officer, who must also be prepared to justify his actions, following any withdrawal, before a court martial'. It was crystal clear that until the reinforcements arrived, every blade of grass, every stone and muddy-mush of land must be fiercely protected. Every man must stand firm at all costs.

The Germans mercilessly bombarded and machine-gunned The Guards at every possible opportunity, day and night. There was no rest from the continual hacking away at their numbers.

It was around this point that one account of astonishing bravery made me gasp when I first came across it. The report was that of Captain Thomas Tannatt Pryce of No 2 Company, 4th Battalion Grenadier Guards.

Fist versus bullet - Death Match

Captain Pryce's company, (a company is about 200 men at full strength), was ordered to attack a village, which was held by Germans. He led two platoons, who worked house to house, killing some thirty enemy soldiers in the process. Seven of them were killed by Captain Pryce alone. The next day they were occupying a position on the battlefield. They were down to thirty or forty men by this time as the rest of his company had either been killed or injured. Early on at around 8.15 a.m., his left flank was surrounded by enemy troops who were enfilading them. This means shooting them in a sweeping action probably with machine-guns. Captain Pryce was attacked no less than four times during the day, and every time his small group of Grenadiers beat off the aggressive charges, killing many of the enemy in the clashes.

Meanwhile the enemy brought up three field guns to within 300 metres of his line, and were firing over open sights. This means they pointed a huge field gun directly at them, rather than them having to work out things like trajectory as they were just so close. Shells from these guns at such short range would have been utterly devastating. This barrage knocked 'seven-bells' out of them and caved in their trench position. At 6.15 p.m., the enemy had worked to within fifty metres of Captain Pryce's trench. Some German troops had also worked their way around and had taken up positions behind them. They were well and truly trapped and this meant they even had to stand back-to-back as they were being shot at from the front and the rear.

Captain Pryce decided to rally his men. There were only thirty alive at this point. He told them to cheer or shout, charge the enemy and fight to the last.

Led by their Captain, they left their trench and drove back the enemy, with their bayonets attached, some 100 metres. Being surrounded worked to their advantage as the Germans were unable to fire on them without occasionally missing and hitting their own soldiers at the rear of Pryce's men. Half an hour later the enemy re-grouped as it had spotted that it was up against the tattered remnants of an isolated, weakened force. With renewed confidence in their task the enemy approached once more. By this time Captain Pryce had only seventeen men left.

What's more they had used up every single round of ammunition. Their guns were therefore useless.

Resolute that there should be no surrender, he once again led his men forward in a bayonet charge. Captain Pryce and his men were last seen fighting hand-to-hand against overwhelming numbers of the enemy who simply surrounded, overwhelmed and consumed them.

Forty men and Captain Pryce had held back at least one enemy battalion (that could be anything up to 1,000 men), for over ten hours!!!

His Company undoubtedly stopped an advance through a fractured, gaping hole in the British line. Accordingly this action had a massive influence on the entire battle.

I don't know about you but this just sums up everything I have ever seen, read, heard and felt about heroism. They were vastly outnumbered, had no ammunition and ended up fighting an overpowering enemy with nothing more than sticks and fists! Unimaginable. There was no surrender, no running away, just plain and simple true grit. Captain Pryce was thirty-two years old when he was killed. He left behind a wife and three young daughters.

He was posthumously awarded the Victoria Cross (VC) for his actions. The Victoria Cross ranks with the George Cross as the nation's highest military award for gallantry. His medal was won for most conspicuous bravery, devotion to duty, and self-sacrifice when in command of the Grenadier Guards.

He has no known grave but his name is commemorated on the Ploegsteert Memorial in Belgium. Captain TT Pryce, I salute you and your valiant crew.

The overall battle continued, with Harry and the brutally battered Guards on the back foot. But they were still hanging in there and most importantly, holding fast.

I wanted to know more about this 'Battle of The Lys' and having spent quite a bit of time reading everything I could about Harry, and the battalions he served in, I was recommended a particular book. It turned out to be three thick books, written by Lieutenant-Colonel The Right Honourable Sir Frederick Ponsonby. I ordered them online and thought, 'they had better be good as it's probably the most expensive set of books I've ever bought'. These books that Ponsonby was tasked with putting together, document the history of the Grenadier Guards during WW1. They were produced using data from numerous war diaries, letters and associated regimental material. They contain a chronological record of all the major events from 1914 to 1918. They are pretty detailed and, I have to say, 'a bit wordy' for me. Well, with a name like Lieutenant-Colonel The Right Honourable Sir Frederick Ponsonby, what would you expect?

The books cover most, if not all, of the key battles and were of particular interest to me as they document the Battle of the Lys from the Grenadiers' perspective.

I was drawn to the information in one of the volumes covering 6 April 1918 onwards, the date Harry returned to the front-line. One section describes an unusual situation, caused by the devastating death-toll and subsequent lack of fighting men. This meant The Guards had to break with tradition and adapt, in the field, to the situation they found themselves in. Harry's 4th Battalion Grenadiers and the 2nd Battalion Coldstream Guards, who had both been heartlessly flattened by the severe fighting, had to combine to make up a 'rag-tag' composite battalion. This had never been done before in the history of the regiments and was obviously due to the fact they had both been virtually wiped out.

Around 18 April, this composite battalion then moved into billets at Le-Tir-Anglais.

One day in Le-Tir-Anglais

On 21 April 1918 Harry sent a letter to Olive as he had done so many times before. It was not much different to any that had gone before and as usual had his address stated in the top right hand corner as follows; 15331, Sergeant Harry Hackett, No 2 Company, 4th Battalion Grenadier Guards, B.E.F., France. However this letter is different from all the rest. It is because it is the last one he ever wrote. Here it is in its entirety;

"My Dearest Wife. At last I am able to write to you a few lines now that I have joined the Battalion as you will see by the above address. I have been worried ever since I left England wondering what has happened to you and whether you and baby got down to Fowey alright or not. It has been impossible for me to write before as we have been on the move ever since last Sunday and I joined the 4th Battalion 2 days ago.

Well Dearest I shall be glad when I can get a letter through from you as you may guess how I have been feeling about you and Dear Baby. It has been a fortnight tonight since we parted and it seems years to me, still so long as you and baby are alright I do not mind.

It does not look like as if I shall have to go into the trenches for a while so I will try and write at every opportunity. You might also write to Old Hill and let them know my address and explain why I have not written I wrote myself and let them know I was out here but could not give them my address so now Dear I shall have to conclude but do not know when this will reach you as it has to be censored.

With fondest and truest love to you and baby, don't forget the kisses from your loving husband Harry xxx".

At the time of writing Harry was not expecting to have to fight so soon. Maybe this was a good thing as the anticipation and apprehension associated with having to face the enemy again would have been reduced. Nonetheless, the war in The Lys was so intense and our lines were haemorrhaging at such a rate of knots, Harry and the men he served with were in the thick of it within a matter of hours.

On 21 April 1918 the composite battalion, mentioned earlier, which included the 4th Battalion Grenadier Guards took over the front line positions from the King's Own Yorkshire Light Infantry. They immediately encountered some intense treatment as the Germans laid down a concentrated, massive bombardment of high explosives and gas shells.

Harry Hackett, died that day. It was a Monday.

During a severe hailstorm of incoming hardware during the battle he had been wounded. After being attended to in the field he would have been transported from the front-line to the 94th Army Field Hospital in Hazebrouck two miles away. Two miles, on a stretcher over a war-torn, mashed up bombsite must have seemed like two months. On reaching the makeshift hospital the medics would have done their best to treat him there along with the deluge of the other poor dying and injured souls.

As he lay in the hospital (or more likely on a stretcher outside) later that day, Harry succumbed to his injuries and passed away. He had been in back in France for just sixteen days.

At just twenty-six years old he had spent a total of 6 years and 293 days serving with The Grenadier Guards. He left behind his wife Olive, their four-month-old son and his family back in The Black Country. As a single parent Olive would be unable to maintain her job in London so at some point she moved to Old Hill to live with Harry's mom and dad. She never remarried and when her son (who was also called Harry) was about 10 years old, they returned home to Fowey to make a new life initially living with her father.

It doesn't bear thinking about does it, being on the receiving end of an airborne-inferno of gas and high explosives. It's a little sickening. It's not surprising that on the same day Harry was fatally wounded, many others were as well. The official 4th Battalion Particulars of Casualties for the period 17 to 25 April 1918 confirms the following:

Raymond Rolfe, Frederick Dean and Richard Dyer were killed in action on 22 April 1918. Harry Hackett along with another colleague Second Lieutenant Raymond Driver Richardson, were also wounded. Harry died later the same day but RD Richardson died four days later at a casualty clearing station half-way between St Omer and Hazebrouck known as Ebblinghem.

There were also nine further casualties that day as well as seventeen poor souls who were listed with the simple, disturbing annotation of 'Gassed'.

Le-Tir-Anglais no longer officially appears on any maps. There are only two or three houses where it would have been. One summer I rode my motorbike through there while on a whistle-stop tour of the area with a good friend of mine. It looked to me very much like any other farm-land area with the usual hedges and ploughed and planted fields. It's very flat and it's hard to imagine it being the hub of a 1918 'Clash of the Titans'.

Harry and his comrades fell in a place that doesn't really exist anymore.

Ironically the fighting on The Lys in 1918, despite causing a short-term crisis for the British army, caused critical damage to the German army. The battle was instrumental in helping to prepare the way for the great Allied counter-attacks that ushered in the last hundred days of the Great War. The Grenadier Guards, and many others, well and truly played their part in this.

'The bad news'

A short Black Country conversation

"Owroit bloke. Ars yar lad doin, I ears th'Hun's geein em a rite lampin bay thay?"

"Ay yo hurd chap?"

"Hurd wha?"

"E bay a cumin hum chap. E copped it in France a Monday wik"

"Yoam jokin. I only sid im a couple a wiks agoo"

"I know, thay was runnin owt o good blokes, sew thay shipped im out. E was only theeya just ova tew wiks. Now e's jed"

"Ar cor belave it mate. Arm sew sorry for yo an the missus".

"E was such a bostin lad, yo culdn't av wanted muwar frum a son. His muthas in bits. Lord elp his wife an the new babbie"

"Lord elp em all mate, Lord elp em all. It's a cryin shame all this war bizniss, tekin all ar yunguns liyke that. Worra bally wairst"

Rest in peace Harry with an H

Today Harry rests in Cinq Rues Cemetery, Hazebrouck, Flanders, Northern France. This could be the exact spot he died because the 94th Field Ambulance station was located there. Harry's headstone bears the Grenadiers emblem of a grenade with seventeen flames near the top and a small crucifix at the bottom. In the middle it simply reads:

> 15331 SERJEANT
>
> H. HACKETT
>
> GRENADIER GUARDS
>
> 22ND APRIL 1918

Every single Commonwealth War Graves Commission (CWGC) grave has a unique location to identify it. Harry's is row B, grave 7.

The site is one of around 2,500 war cemeteries maintained by the CWGC. They maintain the plots, erect headstones and do a fantastic job of honouring our war dead and missing. Their main principles are simple. Each of the dead should be commemorated by name on the headstone or memorial. Headstones and memorials should be permanent. Headstones should be uniform. There should be no distinction made on account of military or civil rank, race or creed.

From the Menin Gate in Ypres, to the mighty Thiepval Memorial in the Somme, through the many memorials in countless towns and cities across our country to the National Memorial in Alrewas, Staffordshire, our armed forces are suitably commemorated and duly celebrated.

You might have noticed that Harry's inscription is just 'H. Hackett' and not 'Harry Hackett'. Most other graves have soldiers' full-names on them, so I thought I'd get this discrepancy put right. I emailed the CWGC people to let them know that I had a little more detail for them regarding the full name. They were very helpful and once they had confirmed who I was and that I was a relative, they were very happy to oblige. They made changes to their database so that it reflected that H was now Harry. Further to that they also included some details

117

regarding his mom and dad and their address in the 'Additional Information' section. This means that whenever anyone searches their records online in the future, they will be a little less ambiguous. This information would have saved me hours of research back when I was first trying to locate the 'right' Harry.

Near Harry's hometown his name and details appear in the book of remembrance at the Rowley Regis War Memorial, Powke Lane just a few minutes' walk from where he grew up as a child.

We shall be heroes

R aymond, Frederick and Richard, the three Grenadiers who died on the same day as Harry, all now lie side by side in Cinq Rues Cemetery.

Lieutenant Raymond Harold Rolfe was the son of Edwin and Harriet Rolfe from Woking, Surrey. Raymond died aged twenty-one. His father Edwin and his older brother Wilfred were military men and were involved in the First World War. Unfortunately, Wilfred was killed in August 1917. He has no known grave but is remembered on panel 96 to 98 at the 'Tyne Cot Memorial to the Missing' just a few miles outside Passchendaele in what was the Ypres Salient. Tyne Cot has 11,954 graves, of which 8,367 contain the remains of unknown soldiers. There are also 101 names of those who were simply never recovered from the battlefield. These all appear, inscribed, on dedicated 'Wall of Memorial' panels.

Raymond now rests next to Harry in row B, grave 6. The inscription on his gravestone reads: "THEY LEAVE BEHIND THEM FAR WORTHIER THINGS THAN TEARS"

Lance Corporal Frederick John Dean MM was the son of Joseph Lavender Dean and Alice Dean, of 2, Princess Avenue, Denton, Manchester. Frederick was born in Ely but the exact date is unknown. He lived in Ely, Cambridgeshire and died aged twenty-one. He was awarded the Military Medal (MM). Frederick won this for an act of gallantry on the night of 19 April 1916, in the Ypres Salient. He volunteered to carry a message back to battalion headquarters, over a distance of half a mile through a heavy barrage. He was successful and brought back an answer to the trenches. He was truly a brave soldier as MM's were never issued lightly. Frederick now rests in row B, grave 8. The gravestone inscription reads: "A YOUNG LIFE GONE HOME WAITING TO MEET AGAIN THE ONES FROM HOME"

Guardsman Richard John Dyer was the son of William and Rachel Dyer and he had a younger sister Rose Marie May (nee Dyer). Richard was born on 28 December 1897. He lived in Broadwell in Oxfordshire a small village in the Cotswolds. Richard died aged twenty, he now rests in row B, grave 9. The inscription on his gravestone reads: "GREATER LOVE HATH NO MAN THAN THIS"

For Harry, Raymond, Richard and Frederick the Great War ended on Monday 22 April 1918. For them the booms of the heavy artillery were silenced that day, machine-guns were void of venom, the deadly gas was just coloured mist on the breeze.

For the rest of the men who survived, the war finally ended after four years, four months and fourteen days at 11:00am on Monday 11 November 1918.

Fifteen million people died during WW1, so it was in every single sense of the word a 'Great War' for every single wrong reason.

1918 was a particularly brutal, savage year for the British Army. They lost more men in the last eleven months of World War One than during the whole of the six years of World War Two (WW2). A sobering and little known fact.

Don't forget to remember the fallen

If you have ever attended a Remembrance Day service anywhere in the world you will probably have read or heard these words;

> *They shall grow not old, as we that are left grow old*
> *Age shall not weary them, nor the years condemn*
> *At the going down of the sun and in the morning*
> *We will remember them*

It's normally read out at some point and everyone 'in the know' joins in on the 'We will remember them' bit. These few lines are actually taken from a longer poem called 'For the Fallen'. It was first published in The Times newspaper on September 21st 1914. It was written by a chap by the name of Laurence Binyon while he was working at the British Museum in London. The poem's fourth verse is now used all over the world during services of remembrance and is inscribed on countless war monuments. The key words that generally linger are, of course, the last four.

Scores of people down the ages have made sure that memories of the brave folks who died serving their countries are honoured especially on 11 November or Armistice Day to use its more formal title. Whenever I've attended any kind of remembrance service I especially reflect on several people, including those in my own and my wife Jacqui's family, who have suffered or died while serving in war-time.

Jacqui lost one of her grandads in 1944. Alfred Watson was killed in Italy during WW2, in what was classed as a Battle Accident, while serving with the 1st Battalion Argyll and Sutherland Highlanders. He rests in a secluded, immaculately kept Commonwealth War Graves cemetery in Faenza, Italy halfway between the city of Bologna and Rimini on the Adriatic coast. Alfred is also remembered, near his home, on a plaque on the Brierley Hill War Memorial located at the top of Church Hill, facing the Clent Hills. Joseph Gwyer, Jacqui's other grandad, served in the Royal Engineers and was captured in the South Pacific whilst on duty. He and his fellow prisoners were marched an inconceivable 1,800 miles on foot from Changi prison in Singapore to Burma. They were then put to work by their Japanese captors as 'forced labour' on the infamous Burmese Railway. In total about 180,000 Asian labourers and 60,000 Allied prisoners of war (POW) worked on what is still referred to as 'The Death Railway'. Of these around 90,000 Asians and 16,000 POWs died as a direct result of working as construction slaves. Joe was imprisoned in one of the notorious Japanese jungle POW camps.

During his latter years he very occasionally mentioned some of the inhuman and cruel treatment he and others received whilst there. It's sometimes beyond words to describe what one man can inflict on another. Joe narrowly, but fortuitously, survived his years of captivity and eventually returned safely to England via the U.S.A. aboard The Queen Mary liner.

At Remembrance time I also give a thought to Rudolf Mausolff the German soldier Harry met. Unfortunately a few months after that moment of Boxing Day peace Rudolf was killed in action. He was a Gefreiter or Lance Corporal in the German army and he died on May 16 1915 at an unknown location.

I normally attend the Remembrance service at Mary Stevens' Park, Stourbridge with Jacqui and a couple of good friends. The first time I ever visited I placed a small wooden cross and a poppy at the foot of the memorial there. I noticed that the War Memorial had been vandalised with paint. I suppose kids just don't know what it represents and couldn't care less. I'd like to think I'd be the last person to judge, and when you understand yourself why the memorial is there and what it stands for it's terrible to see something like that corrupted for absolutely no point whatsoever. I guess it's just a lesson that we should educate the young. If they don't know what a 'weird pointy stone structure with initials and names on' means then what's to stop them treating it like a blank urban canvas for valueless graffiti?

Poppy power

A few years ago I was asked to help sell poppies as part of the British Legion Poppy Appeal. It's something the firm I work for does every year to support their wider corporate and social responsibilities. I was very happy to oblige and have since volunteered every November. Before I found out I had any military links I generally bought a poppy but didn't really engage or connect whole-heartedly with the whole remembrance thing. I'd certainly make sure I kept the two minutes silence on Armistice Day (if I could, well, your mind wanders doesn't it?) but that was about it. Nowadays Remembrance Day is a key date on the Rudall family calendar. We all, in our own ways, make sure we honour the dead and injured as well as remember the lost from our own family.

I suppose like a lot of people I generally feel uncomfortable asking for money even if it's for a good cause but when it comes to selling poppies you don't need to even try. You just 'make yourself seen' with your little tray of poppies hanging neatly around your neck and your bright red-plastic collection tin. Folks make a bee-line for you. It's quite a privilege and a great thing to be involved in. People making donations grab a poppy from the tray, carefully fumble for the all-important pin and in so doing know that they are supporting something worthy and right. I love selling poppies and I love what they stand for.

There is nothing great about war. Its fuel is death and pain and it belches out bones and blood. But it is good to remember the fallen of any war. More than that, we have a duty to remember those who have been consumed by wars fought in our name. I will continue to encourage anyone who will listen to support Armistice Day simply by wearing a poppy and taking time to stop and think at 11am on the 11th of the 11th month. It's important. Without it lessons of the past are lost, meaning, God forbid, mistakes of the past might get a sequel.

So is it true when they say, The Show Must Go On?

I often ask myself, 'what has changed since that day in Le-Tir-Anglais?' While I was writing this section of this book my phone warbled in my pocket. It was a text from a BBC news alert service I subscribe to. It read as follows:

> *From: 82002*
>
> *Sent: Nov 4, 2009 07:46*
>
> *Subject: BBC NEWS: Five British soldiers...*
>
> *BBC NEWS: Five British soldiers have been killed in an attack in Afghanistan, the Ministry of Defence says. Next of kin have been informed.*

It's an all too common message of recent times. Our troops serving in the Middle East and Afghanistan are at the sharp end, they are in harm's way. I have to be honest in saying that I think that today, the pressures of modern life, the relative comfort of our 'i-Everything' existence mean that messages like this sometimes just bounce off the surface of our lives. We hear the names of those lost, we generally hear very little detail of how they died. I'm sad to say we generally just don't understand, it's all very distant and vague.

Quite by coincidence three of the five soldiers were from the Grenadier Guards. This detail however made me take particular note.

In numerous TV interviews with loved ones later that day I heard the following tributes; 'a wonderful lad, a model soldier, a true brother, you couldn't have asked for a better son, a consummate professional, absolutely loved, a cheeky smile, mourned by a loving family, leaves a wife and two kids'. They are simple, almost predictable, words but they are also deep and heartfelt. They are the truth. They are the immediate, honest response to loss. They are voiced to sum up the vast hidden-characteristics and precious-personalities of each life lost. Words clamber and struggle in an attempt to express feelings that are buried deep within those left behind. They go far beyond any language that any man can utter. They are timeless words that could have been expressed with equal sorrow by the family Harry Hackett left behind all those years ago.

Closer to home I am reminded of a young man whom I have thought about many, many times since I first discovered my links with Harry and the Grenadier Guards. There are several key factors that account for this. He was just a few years older than my own son. His mom worked at the same care home as my wife Jacqui. He was from Tipton just a few miles from Old Hill in the West Midlands. He was attached to the exact same regiment Harry served in. And, he was killed while serving his country, just like Harry.

This young man was a Guardsman in the 1st Battalion Grenadier Guards. His name was Daniel Probyn. He was a Black Country Grenadier.

At just 22 years old this young man tragically lost his life. Daniel was part of a night patrol tasked with clearing a Taliban compound on the outskirts of Garmsir, a deadly Taliban controlled area, in Southern Helmand Province, Afghanistan. He, along with the twenty four men of 3 Platoon, left their Forward Operating Base (FOB) around an hour before midnight on 25 May 2007. Their task was to mount an aggressive assault and destroy a Taliban outpost that was being used to menace the FOB with deadly rocket-propelled grenades. The outpost, that was only half a mile from the FOB, needed to be 'dealt with'. As the team made their way along a shallow trench, under cover of darkness, the order was given to attach bayonets. This was because this very same ditch was known to be used, from time to time, as a 'rat-run' by Taliban fighters. They needed to be 'on their game' and prepared for anything. When they reached the compound, machine-gun fire and hand grenade 'thuds' began filling the air as the team worked their way through the area clearing the Taliban positions. It was at this point that a simple pressure-switch detonated an Improvised Explosion Device (IED). It's reported that a blinding, incandescent, white light from the blast lit up the surrounding area. This cowardly 'human-mousetrap', had triggered the devastating explosion. It killed Daniel instantly.

Seconds before the detonation a fundamental life-saving act occurred. Daniel, who was 'on point' with a group of fellow Guardsmen, had assessed the precarious situation with great caution and skill. I doubt that anyone can imagine anything quite as threatening as being on patrol, viewing the grainy-green world through night-vision goggles on foot, at the dead of night, in an 'IED-infested' Taliban controlled area. Thinking on his feet, and calling on his training and considerable battle experience gained from previous tours of duty, he made a vital, life-saving decision. His group was tightly bunched so he simply made sure the other lads in his patrol had 'fanned' out to cover more ground and importantly to ensure they didn't present more of a target. This astute combat judgment minimised any potential threat and seconds later it saved the lives of four Guardsmen who were to his immediate right and left.

The blast was a 'biggie' and even though the four lads with him were saved they received serious injuries. Guardsman Scott Blaney had his right leg torn off and sustained major damage to his right arm and eye. Lance Corporal Nick Davis also lost a leg and Corporal Paul Morgan and Guardsman Ashley O'Sullivan suffered extensive shrapnel wounds. In the melee the rest of the platoon responded immediately by returning fire to secure the area so they could respond to their shattered colleagues. The casualties were quickly but cautiously removed, as the incident had escalated to a serious conflict, to a safe area where they would rendezvous with a Chinook helicopter. One of the lads was even hauled, for a mile, over a Drill Sergeant's shoulder to ensure they were well out of the kill zone as soon as humanly possible.

My story about Harry and his experiences are distant in comparison to this. There's no one left who was there at the time to tell his story. It was a different era and of course it was almost 100 years ago. The incident with Daniel is, relatively speaking, still very much in the 'here and now'. It is very physical as the pain and loss are still very tangible to those close to him.

Daniel joined the Army in 2003 and in the few years following he served in Iraq as part of Operation (Op) TELIC 5 and Op TELIC 8. TELIC was the codename that signified British military operations in Iraq between the start of the Invasion of Iraq on 19 March 2003 and the final withdrawal of our forces on 22 May 2011. During this time Daniel received a, 'much played down by him', commendation for assisting with the evacuation of an injured soldier whilst under sustained attack. Back home he loved his motorcycles and was a dedicated West Bromwich Albion fan. According to those who served with him he was extremely popular and very well respected within his Platoon. He will remain in their eyes, without doubt, a legend.

Through the contact of a close personal friend I was very kindly invited by Daniel's parents, Ann and Tim Probyn, to meet with them for a chat. It was something I've wanted to do ever since I realised the link between Harry and Daniel a couple of years ago. I was very moved to be invited to see the many, extremely personal, possessions and mementos of their son's life. It was more than obvious that these two people were still very affected by their loss. His memory is celebrated and appreciably physical in their home. Daniel was, and is, very precious to them and their immediate family. Initially I felt like I was invading their privacy at times but this dispersed as we got to know each other and shared stories. With the obvious common bond we rattled on for hours about The Grenadier Guards, war, Harry and Daniel.

During my time with Ann and Tim I was very kindly allowed to flick through a bunch of unofficial private photographs of the 1st Battalion taken by Daniel's fellow Guardsmen. Some show them chilling out in their camp, others while they were in action. They depict scenes of up-to-date army life like nothing I've ever seen before. They really give a feel for how it is out there and in particular the live combat pictures made the hairs on the back of my neck stand on end. More than that there was something even more striking about a few of the 'action' images that I just have to mention. One or two photographs, that are almost black and white due to the light conditions, made me do a 'double-take'. During my research I must have seen hundreds of WW1 combat snapshots with Tommies standing at the parapet of their trench ducking incoming fire and returning the odd shot from their rifles. One particular image in the collection was of a group of Guardsmen right in the thick of it. For the first few seconds of looking I honestly thought it was a WW1 photograph. It shows half a dozen or so Guardsmen, some standing at a makeshift parapet-like wall, shooting at the enemy. Some are crouched nearby on standby ready to take over from those shooting once they'd emptied their magazines. There was smoke and dust and bits of flying debris everywhere. Maybe it was the monochrome appearance of the photograph, nevertheless, to me, it bore an uncanny resemblance to a WW1 battle scene.

The similarity of that snapshot-situation, frozen in time, was something I never ever expected to see in the context of our modern-day warfare. Seeing 21st century Guardsmen standing in lines in trench-like conditions facing an enemy head on was a complete shock to me. The vast majority of mainstream TV and media footage in my experience depicts current battle action as almost clinical and detached from the reality of real infantry combat. The image opened my eyes, it told a very different story.

Daniel's name appears on a new bronze plaque on the existing War Memorial in Steven's Park near Quarry Bank. His name also appears on the walls of the very impressive and poignant National Memorial Arboretum.

Soldiers still face death on our behalf on a daily basis and they do this without question and without flinching. They do their job. They honour their country, their regiments and their families. Some like Harry and Daniel pay the ultimate price. We should all continue to fully support and adequately equip our troops abroad as if they were our own sons and daughters. After all they 'step into the breach' and wage war so that we, and those they are protecting, can live in peace.

As I write this section the 1st Battalion Grenadier Guards are currently preparing to return to Afghanistan as part of Op HERRICK 16. So it seems, after all that, 'The Show' does indeed go on.

An uncomplicated hope

Over the past few years I've visited the spot where Harry rests in Northern France in all seasons and in all types of weather. I know it's 'a graveyard' but I don't find it grim or sinister at all. To me it's a place of colour and life. It's also a place that at one time I'd have never in this world expected to find myself visiting. I've spent quiet times sitting by the precisely engraved, white Portland headstone, just looking, thinking, letting my mind wander as I gaze up at blue skies. The occasional wreath of red poppies or bunch of flowers breaks up the neatly turned soil. I've felt the damp green grass and soft earth beneath my feet, gazed out at the surrounding fields, hedges and trees, thinking of the same place but at a different time. I have contemplated the 'neat little rows' of names and numbers. I have felt the eager breeze on my face that almost unremittingly attempts to nag its guests 'not to forget'. I have allowed myself to listen; I have breathed that place in.

To me it is a place of peace and a place of purpose and a place of promise.

Harry Hackett, The Black Country Grenadier, is my hero. My uncomplicated hope is that in some way his memory would continue, in some small way to live on, and just make people think about life, love and what we have, instead of what we don't have. After all a wise man once said…'Greater love has no man than this that he lay down his life for his friends'.

Don't forget that not a single word of this book would have been written if it were not for a complete and utter, quite by chance, occurrence in a charity shop in 2009. In life, you never know what is around the corner for you. I never ever imagined I'd ever write a book. But, as I always tell my kids, 'never say never'. It's strange how some things come to be.

Finally, thank you for reading this book and in doing so being part of Harry's and my story. And, if you are ever in Harry's neck of the woods, pop in and see him and his pals. You never know, you might even find me there.

EPILOGUE

So, what on God's earth was it like to go over the top?

Over the top or OTT is used these days as a simple phrase to convey something that's excessive or overdone. In the context of WW1 these three words had a completely unique implication. At one end of the spectrum it simply means what it says, that is, physically climbing and going over the top of the parapet in order to cross no-man's-land and attack the enemy. At the other end it was a command that was, if disobeyed, the equivalent of writing your own suicide note. There was only one way to escape following this command and that was a bullet from one of your own men who were specifically tasked with shooting anyone who failed to comply. In order to offer a 'micro-glimpse' into what it meant to obey this order I wrote the following fictional account. It's my hope that this may, in some small way, shed a little light on the matter. Everything you read in the next few paragraphs is a re-written composite of some of the many accounts I've read from survivors of the First World War. The chain of events are 'made up' but the links are based on the truth. It's a stream of consciousness or inner monologue from the perspective of what might be going on in a young man's head just before and after he went 'over the top'.

Every one of my senses is turned up to ten. I can hear my heart beating, it feels like it's trying to escape through my chest. I can't stop shivering and quivering from fear, my teeth occasionally chatter, my mouth is dry, my eyes are wide. We're all at attention, bayonets fixed, standing in the mud and slop at the bottom of our man-made gash created by hand, in the French soil. We face the seven-foot wall of our hidey-hole. It's around dawn, a bit chilly and the morning mist hangs and extends its ghostly fingers out into no-man's-land. There is no sun, not today. It is probably better off hidden behind the clouds that way it will not have to witness what is about to take place.

Some 'smart Alec' down the line makes a joke, I don't quite catch it. I just hear a few subdued, nervous laughs. Everyone avoids eye contact. Breathing is sharp and staccato. I've checked my kit, as they told me to. Belts, buckles, bullets and bombs. I steal a quick peek at my sweetheart's photograph before it's slipped back into the pocket closest to my heart. The lad next to me is singled out by our Sergeant and told, 'You son! Stay in this trench! If any of these men come back down these ladders for any reason other than because I've have asked them to, YOU WILL SHOOT THEM where they stand! That is an order! Is that clear?' The lad's face is a picture; fear, loathing, disbelief. He has now been promoted to an executioner in waiting.

We are all as 'ready as we'll ever be', except that we don't want to 'be'. In front of me is a cheap excuse for a ladder that will quite possibly provide me with first-class passage to heaven via hell. I focus on its bottom step which will be my starting block. As I stare, looking past it rather than at it, I notice that someone has in a moment of boredom or devilment carved 'STAIRWAY TO HEAVEN' on it.

Very soon I will be propelled by a corporate wave that will see us all dash in a robotic-half-trance towards everything that wants to snuff us out. My toes are freezing cold but at this moment I don't mind because it reminds me that I am still alive.

Our Captain walks down the line past his men, his head is down his expression blank. He stares at his watch, checks the time and looks up at the parapet. Did I spot a millisecond of doubt? No, surely not. He goes for his whistle and purposefully places it between his salt-stained dry lips. Another quick check of his watch and I see him draw a long breath. I don't even hear the whistle, I just see his cheeks bulge and blast. I sense movement on both sides. My cold right foot hits the bottom step of the ladder, we are off! It's 'show-time'.

The whistle, like the tap of a conductor's baton, has unleashed the orchestra of the gods. There are so many sounds and at such volume that all I hear is an amalgamated deep wail as if nature is groaning, begging us to stop. It amplifies as if every noise ever articulated was being replayed at precisely the same time. I'm deafened by my own ability to hear. The dull 'thwack' of bullets hitting the ground in front of me grabs my attention, the man next to me drops like an anvil. I catch his lifeless dead eye a split second before he hits the ground where he is embraced by the malevolent mud.

The sounds that surround me begin to separate; I hear explosions all around and shatters from the sky as shrapnel shells dispatch red hot shards of death from above. The deep, constantly throbbing heavy guns launch shells over my head directed at our intended target. Our intended target retaliates like-for-like. We press on, bent double, zigzagging our barbed wire, splintered tree stumps, shell holes and heaps of new as well as old bodies. We use faces, necks and chests as stepping stones, it's impossible to avoid them. We are all constantly listening for the tap-tap-tap sweep of machine-gun fire. Suddenly the rapid rhythm of the tap-tap-tap turns to a dull 'hammer-like' thud-thud-thud for a second as it slashes the man to my left clean in two at waist height. I dive to the floor transfixed as the man's legs take two final steps forwards minus a torso. I am sickened but that feeling is pushed to the back of my mind as I deal with making myself as small and compact as possible to avoid the bullets now whizzing inches from my prone, unmoving body.

The 'inner me' kicks in and I'm processing a thousand thoughts, sounds and feelings at the same time. I have to stay low, I have to keep advancing, it is why I am here. The snapping bullets continue to hiss as they cut through the air all around me. I catch a glance again at the 'man in two'. I count the gaps between the machine-gun strafes that rake across the killing field from left to right and then back again. I have an exit plan, during one of the gaps, as the bullets sweep from left to right, I bolt upright and with superhuman strength, explode out of my shallow temporary cover. Up ahead through the dust, smoke and debris I see the enemy. I aim, while still running and fire off shot after shot. My aim is 'all over the place', I'm probably only killing thin air. All around me men are rushing forwards in spurts. Some are falling, some silently, some with shrieks of pain. I am a player on Hell's pitch. I am off-side. I don't want to be here.

They didn't tell me it would be like this. How could they? No one would have ever believed them. Again more machine-gun fire traces its way towards me. I see the effects of bullets hitting men, splitting timber and splashing in puddles and mud. It's coming my way again. Before the 'snake' reaches me and before I have time to react, the scene around me changes. It's suddenly dead quiet. Time appears to freeze. Every colour is richer and more vivid. There's a throbbing brightness and several pin-points of light sparkle like diamonds. Then, 'boom', time returns to normal. Pain times one thousand is focussed in my right shin. My immediate thoughts are that I've been hit by a hammer. I'm falling down. Oh God, I'm down. I'm gulping, my face contorts. I'm flat on my face and suddenly my head is under mud and water. I can't breathe. I can't see. There's a weight bearing down on me forcing me deeper into my 'mud-mask'. I'm sucking in mud. My panic powers me and I wriggle for all I'm worth to my right. For a second my face is free of the suffocation. I gulp in a lung full of air. The dead-weight on me is a 'dead-weight'. It's a fallen soldier. The pain in my shin shoots electrical spasms through me making me jump. I mouth a cry but I'm incapable of reaching the crescendo of a scream. I heave the dead man off of me as he's trying to drown me even in death. As I push him off me he showers me with the contents of his head. It's warm. It's in my eyes, it runs down my neck, I can taste his death. No sooner am I free he becomes my shelter and my shield. His lifeless body is between me and the snaking machine-guns, he is absorbing bullet after bullet. The sharp thud as metal finds flesh and bone is appalling; he is a temporary bullet shelter.

I catch fast breaths, I'm scared stiff but again the 'inner me' is working out options and calculating plans for freedom. Can I get up? Can I walk? Can I get some field dressing on my wound? Do I have a leg? If I move an inch I will find myself a sitting target for enemy shooters, so I wait. The situation wants to beat me, so I just 'suck it up'. The pain renders me immobile, there is no way I can walk. I sit tight, corpse-like, except that I have the all important beating heart. I'm just listening and thinking. Bullets continue to zip, what seem like inches from my head. I can't see what's going on around me as I'm face down staring at the dirt that we are all dying for. Terrified to twitch my head to take a look at what's going on around me, I focus on my breathing. I must calm down. My ears are my only advisor. My head spins.

It's suddenly darker and much, much quieter. I think I must have blacked-out. I panic as I try to re-start my thinking and pick up where I left off.

The sounds of battle are gone and have been replaced with an eerie, flat silence. I hesitate and lift my head ever so slowly to get my bearings. I can't make any shapes out that might help me understand where I am. Where is our trench? Is it behind me or in front of me? I check the pain in my shin, it's numb but strangely bearable until I try to move. I muffle my own cries with the back of my sleeve but I still hear a scream. I'm sure I covered my mouth, no wait, it wasn't me screaming. It was a fellow about a stones-throw away. I listen. There it is again, a whimper, a cry and short gasps obviously borne of severe pain. He is calling out, he is begging. He calls for his 'mother' over and over. His pitiful pain and persistent petitioning make me wince with sympathy. This symphony of suffering goes on for ages. It's agonizing and almost unbearable to listen to a man in that state, especially one you are powerless to help. Out of the blue I hear the crisp crack of a single rifle shot. I don't hear the man again after that.

I sober myself into action, I make my mind be 'alert'. I decide that I have to move, I have to survive. I start to half crawl and occasionally roll, it's my only method of transport. When I catch my shin the pain rockets through me and stabs my brain. I keep rolling and crawling, rolling and crawling. I slide through mud, dirt, over barbed wire and the shredded debris and contents of men. The stench and body-parts make me gag, I don't care, I block it out. The disgust and discomfort motivates me to press on and continue to exist.

Suddenly I hear voices and then the occasional gunshot. The voices are not English, it is the enemy. I freeze, and try to pin-point them. They are coming from the location of where I fell. I'm heading away from them so I must be going in the right direction. I wait. Then roll. I wait then roll. I wait...I hear more voices. They are closer this time. Thank God, they are not enemy voices. In the inky darkness I can hardly see anything as there is no light and no moon. But I see shapes moving towards me, I hear the squelch and sucking sounds of boots in mud. I see two men, they are the silhouettes of salvation. I call out with the volume of a church mouse. They don't hear. I try again and again. Finally they hear. I call out 'Don't shoot, help me please?' In pitch blackness they gingerly pick their way through wire entanglements and step on and over men who are now beyond help. Eventually they reach me. I'm dragged onto a stretcher.

We are on the home straight, except that the enemy are looking for us. They'd like nothing more than to pick us off like ducks on a fairground shooting range. My saviours stumble with the weight of their cargo on the unstable, uneven wet surface. We all see the tracer of a flare fired from a pistol nearby, in seconds it will be directly above us lighting up no-man's-land like it's daytime. We crash to the floor and lock in place. Any movement and we will be the focus of opportunistic enemy fire. The pain as we hit the deck makes the toes on my good foot curl. I bite through my lip and stifle a burbling cry of pain. The flare slowly dies out, we wait a second or two and then resume our trek.

I hold on to the stretcher for dear life, muffling the odd squeak caused by the intense pain, through gritted teeth. I don't care about my transporters' lack of care. I want to go home.

Finally we are in one of our trenches. It's dark, damp and cold. To me, at this moment, it is a palace. They place me on the sodden duckboards on the floor of my sanctuary. I say a quick 'thank you' to God and man. My saviours are off to find more like me. Lying down, my head rolls to one side as I contemplate the last few hours. In my relief I exhale a long, deep breath and slowly open my eyes. Out of the darkness at the bottom of the trench several awkward, jagged, carved letters come into focus. I immediately recognise them. I reach out with my fingers as I trace out the word 'HEAVEN'.

Andrew Mark Rudall *(Andy)*

FACTS AND FIGURES

Army Service Record Dates For Harry Hackett

Location	From	To	Years	Days
Home	03/07/11	03/10/14	3	93
Western Front	04/10/14	29/03/16	1	76
Home	29/03/16	05/03/18	2	18
Western Front	06/04/18	22/04/18	-	16
Total			**6**	**293**

Note: 'Home' may refer to either serving in England or recovering from injury

First World War Casualty Figures

Country	Mobilised	Dead	Wounded	Missing/POW
Germany	11,000,000	1,773,700	4,216,058	1,152,800
Russia	12,000,000	1,700,000	4,950,000	2,500,000
France	8,410,000	1,375,800	4,266,000	537,000
Austria-Hungary	7,800,000	1,200,000	3,620,000	2,200,000
GB & Empire	8,904,467	908,371	2,090,212	191,652

THE BROTHERS IN ARMS

From left to right; Raymond, Harry, Frederick and Richard of the 4th Battalion Grenadier Guards

The 'Neat Little Rows'

RIP - LIEUTENANT RAYMOND HAROLD ROLFE

4th Battalion Grenadier Guards

Date of birth unknown – 22 April 1918

Raymond now rests in row B, grave 6

RIP - SERGEANT HARRY HACKETT
15331

1st and later 4th Battalion Grenadier Guards

3 January 1981 – 22 April 1918

Harry now rests in row B, grave 7

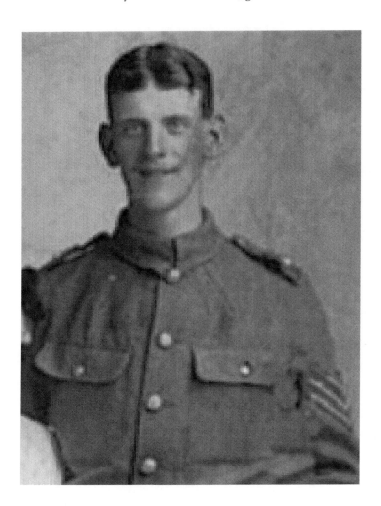

RIP - LANCE CORPORAL FREDERICK JOHN DEAN MM

4th Battalion Grenadier Guards

DOB unknown – 22 April 1918

Frederick now rests in row B, grave 8

RIP - GUARDSMAN RICHARD JOHN DYER

4th Battalion Grenadier Guards

28 December 1897 – 22 April 1918

Richard now rests in row B, grave 9

MEMORIAL CASE AND MEDALS

Centre top: Harry's original NCO's cap badge

Centre middle: Harry's medals. The 1914 Star, the Britsh War Medal and the Victory Medal. A bar clasp inscribed 5 Aug. to 22 Nov. 1914 was given to all those who qualified for the 1914 Star and who served under fire. The medals were affectionately known by our troops as 'Pip, Squeak and Wilfred'.

Centre bottom: Memorial Plaque

MEMORIAL PLAQUE

The Memorial Plaque was issued after the First World War to the next-of-kin of all British and Empire service personnel who were killed as a result of the war. The plaques were about 120mm or 5 inches in diameter, made of bronze, and hence popularly known as the 'Dead Man's Penny', because of the similarity in appearance to the somewhat smaller penny coin. 1,355,000 plaques were issued. This one was awarded to Mrs Olive Doretta Hackett, Harry's widow.

The plaque shows; an image of Britannia holding a trident and an oak spray with leaves and acorns; an imperial lion; two dolphins; representing Britain's sea power; the emblem of Imperial Germany's eagle being torn to pieces by another lion; a rectangular tablet showing HARRY HACKETT in raised lettering. No rank was given as it was intended to show equality in their sacrifice, the words, 'HE DIED FOR FREEDOM AND HONOUR'. The memorial plaque would be accompanied with a Memorial Scroll, a letter from Buckingham Palace and often a letter from the deceased's commanding officer. They would not usually arrive as a single package, but as a series of separate mailings.

SOME OF 'THE LETTERS'

The birthday card Harry made for Olive's 21st birthday whilst he was on the Western Front

A SELECTION OF LETTERS AND POSTCARDS

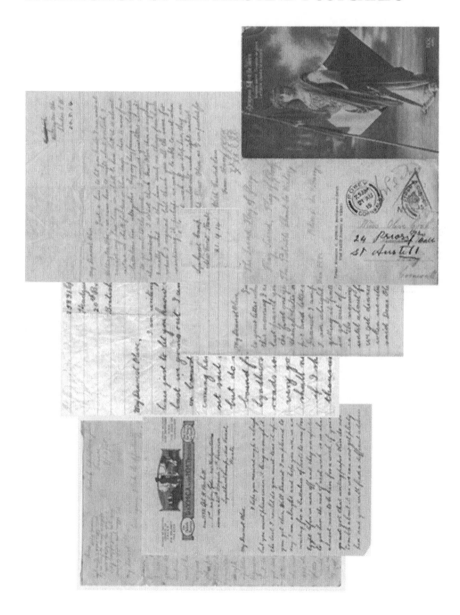

THE FIRST PAGE OF HARRY'S LAST LETTER TO OLIVE DATED 21 APRIL 1918

AN EXAMPLE OF HOW HARRY USUALLY ENDED ALL HIS
LETTERS TO OLIVE

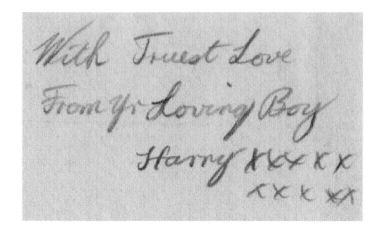

ONE OF HARRY'S LETTERS WRITTEN WHILST ON YMCA
HEAEDED PAPER WAITING FOR ORDERS TO 'GO TO THE
FRONT' AT LYNHURST CAMP

THE WAR MEMORIAL

Powke Lane Cenotaph, Rowley Regis, West Midlands

Harry's details are recorded on the Rowley Regis Council Roll of Honour. A copy is kept at Powke Lane Cenotaph which is less than half a mile from where Harry lived in Old Hill.

PLACES AND POPPIES

Above; The Grote Markt, Ypres. Below; The Menin Gate at night

A wreath at the Menin Gate left by The Wordsley School, Stourbridge

'A poppy seller's point of view'. At Snowhill Station, Birmingham 2010

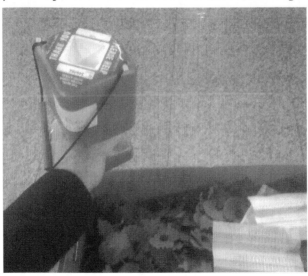

BLACK COUNTRY TRANSLATIONS

'Joining up' – Black Country version

1. "Owbin ya me owd taerter?"

2. *"Bay ter bad. Ars yerself chap?"*

3. "Bostin, omma jiynen th'armay bay I"

4. *"Yow, bay bin ya?"*

5. "Ar bin, omma jiynen the Grenadiers an all"

6. *"Well I be bloed. Ar bet tha fairthers chuffed aye e?"*

7. "Ar. E sez I shaw bi no wuss off than I bin eya. An itul be ova afower Krismuss woe et?"

8. *"Cors et ull, cocker. Any road I cor stop a cantin I best be gooin. Yo tek care mi mon an keep yer yed dowen"*

9. "I sholl"

10. *"Tararabit"*

11. "Tarar chap"

'Joining up' – English version

1. "How are you old pal?"

2. *"Not bad at all, how about you?"*

3. "I'm doing great, in fact I'm joining the army"

4. *"You don't say?"*

5. "Yes I am. I'm joining the Grenadiers"

6. *"Well who would have thought it. I would imagine your father is really pleased about that?"*

7. "He certainly is and he says that I won't be any worse off than I am here at home. Plus it will be well over before Christmas won't it?"

8. *"Of course it will my friend. Anyway, I'm afraid I can't talk at the moment I better be on my way. Take good care of yourself and keep your head down"*

9. "I certainly will"

10. *"See you soon"*

11. "Good bye"

'The short visit home' - Black Country version

1. "Owbin ya mi mon? I bay sid yer fer yonks"

2. *"I bin ova theyar fightin aye I, and I bay doin' ter good bloke"*

3. "Ow come?"

4. *"On jus come back frum tha frunt aye I. W'een ad a good thraypin off the Bosch an all?"*

5. "Wan ya dun ter yer fairce mi mon?"

6. *"We waz in a scrap an a shell cum ova as big as a bonk 'oss. I gorrit a cockaver. I wan lucky though it neely took mi yed off"*

7. "Am yo finished wi fightin now then chap?"

8. *"No chonce. I gorruw goo back as soon as this un's eeled. Thayme short on blokes owt theyar, thay naydes all th'elp thay con get"*

9. "It doe sarnd ter good mate"

10. *"It aye mate, it's murder mate"*

11. "Lord elp ya mi mon"

12. *"Ta chap...an do us a faver will ya...pray for us mate"*

13. "Wi bin me owd taerter, dow thee werrit abart that'

'The short visit home' – English version

1. "How are you my friend? I say I haven't seen you for quite some time"

2. *"I know, I've been abroad fighting and I'm afraid I'm not doing so well"*

3. "What's the matter?"

4. *"I've just returned from the front. The German army has really been giving us a good beating?"*

5. "Whatever have you done to your face?"

6. *"We were in a fire-fight and a huge shell the size of a horse landed nearby. I caught the blast and was very lucky it didn't take my head clean off"*

7. "Does that mean you won't be returning to active duty again?"

8. *"That's very unlikely. I'm due to return as soon as this injury has healed. We are really short on fighting men, they need all the help they can get"*

9. "That doesn't sound too good at all my friend"

10. *"It's not, it's nothing less than murder"*

11. "Lord help you"

12. *"Thank you…and could I ask a favour?…would you pray for us please?"*

13. "We are my friend, don't you worry about that".

'The bad news' - Black Country version

1. "Owroit bloke. Ars yar lad doin, I ears th'Hun's geein em a rite lampin bay thay?"

2. *"Ay yo hurd chap?"*

3. "Hurd wha?"

4. *"E bay a cumin hum chap. E copped it in France a Monday wik"*

5. "Yoam jokin. I only sid im a couple a wiks agoo"

6. *"I know, thay was runnin owt o good blokes, sew thay shipped im out. E was only theeya just ova tew wiks. Now e's jed"*

7. "Ar cor belave it mate. Arm sew sorry for yo an the missus".

8. *"E was such a bostin lad, yo culdn't av wanted muwar frum a son. His muthas in bits. Lord elp his wife an the new babbie"*

9. "Lord elp em all mate, Lord elp em all. It's a cryin shame all this war bizniss, tekin all ar yunguns liyke that. Worra bally wairst"

'The bad news' – English version

1. "Hello. How is your son doing by the way? I hear that the Germans are giving our lads a real hiding?"

2. *"Have you not heard?"*

3. "Heard about what?"

4. *"He isn't coming home. He was killed a week last Monday in France"*

5. "Please tell me you are kidding? I only saw him just a couple of weeks ago"

6. *"I know, the army were running out of fighting men so they shipped him out there. He was only there just over two weeks. Now he is dead"*

7. "I can't believe it. I am so sorry for you and your wife"

8. *"He was such a lovely young man, you could not have asked for more from a son. His mother is beside herself. Lord help his wife and the new born baby"*

9. "Lord help them all, Lord help them all. It's a crying shame, all this warfare taking all our young lads just like that. What an absolute waste"

GUARDSMAN DANIEL PROBYN

1st Battalion Grenadier Guards

7 October 1984 – 26 May 2007

Daniel in action with his GPMG

The 'thousand yard' stare

In the thick of it – real 'Modern Warfare'

In active duty gear and his formal Guardsman uniform with bearskin

ABOUT THE AUTHOR

Andy is a 'Black Country' lad who decided one day to write down his experiences to ensure the remarkable circumstances and discovery of his World War One Uncle were not lost. His journey of learning and understanding is written in a very informal conversational style with the intention that it is endearing, informative and easy to read.

Andy lives in Amblecote, West Midlands with his wife Jacqui, son Adison and daughter Holli. They share their home with their two beloved Shih Tzu's, Booi and Radley as well as Andy's much-loved Chihuahua called Diddle.

Until the almost insignificant events early in 2009 that cascaded into the publication of this book, Andy had no interest at all in world history, let alone the four short years of World War One. Even though he would be the first to admit that he is not a specialist on the subject by any stretch of the imagination he has developed a passion for that short and defining period in our history and heritage.

Andy is extremely proud of his Black Country heritage and to be associated with Harry, The Grenadier Guards and all those who serve their country selflessly.

FURTHER INFORMATION SOURCES

The Colonel's Fund Grenadier Guards – www.thecolonelsfund.com

Help for Heroes – www.helpforheroes.org.uk

CWGC – www.cwgc.org

In Flanders Fields Museum - www.inflandersfields.be

The Long, Long Trail - www.1914-1918.net

The Great War Forum – www.1914-1918.invisionzone.com

The Grenadier Guards – www.grengds.com

The Black Country Living Museum - www.bclm.co.uk

The Black Country Bugle - www.blackcountrybugle.co.uk

Sergeant Harry Hackett - www.neatlittlerows.co.uk

WHY...?

Kill	War	Worry	Crawl	Save
Run	Fall	Hear	Throw	Hit
Stab	Help	Carry	Hurt	Breathe
Look	Cry	Smoke	Hide	Wait
Go	Shoot	Drown	Suffer	March
Think	Write	Dig	Stare	Salute
Watch	Exist	Obey	Witness	Bother
Wonder	Laugh	Stay	Read	Me
Sweat	Hope	Fight	Pray	Die
		Forgive		

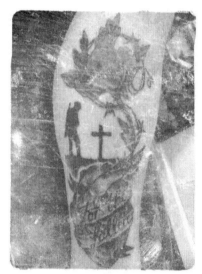